BASIC ABILITIES:
A WHOLE APPROACH

HUMAN HORIZONS SERIES

BASIC ABILITIES:
A WHOLE APPROACH

A Developmental Guide for Children with Disabilities

Written and illustrated by
SOPHIE LEVITT

A CONDOR BOOK
SOUVENIR PRESS (E&A) LTD

First published 1994 by Souvenir Press (Educational & Academic) Ltd,
43 Great Russell Street, London WC1B 3PD
and simultaneously in Canada

Reprinted in 2002

ISBN 0 285 63171 3

Printed in Great Britain by St Edmundsbury Press Ltd,
Bury St Edmunds, Suffolk

CONTENTS

ACKNOWLEDGEMENTS

During the years in which my ideas have been developing I have had useful discussions with a number of colleagues. I thank them all, especially Dr Pam Zinkin, Dr Patricia Sonksen, the late Mary Kitzinger, Lesley Carroll and Katrin Stroh. David Halpern has been most helpful in preparing and typing the manuscript. Thanks also to Maureen Griffiths for comments and typing. My students on various workshops have stimulated me and assisted me in crystallising my ideas, and for this I am most grateful. My thanks go to the Swedish parent organisations RBU for physical handicap, FUB for mental handicap and SRF for severe visual handicap. They kindly commissioned me to write a book on my approach for Swedish parents and carers. This book has developed from it and is more extensive and detailed. Finally, my thanks to all the parents and children for giving me the privilege of working with them and learning with them.

S.L.

PREFACE

The ideas in this book have grown out of many years of work with parents and their children who have disabilities and special needs. They have been helped by many different professionals, in medicine, education and social work, and I have drawn on the work of all these disciplines in order to treat child and parent as a whole, from their viewpoint.

This has meant learning what I could from the valuable contributions of my colleagues in a number of countries. I am therefore grateful to the numerous professionals who have given me generously of their knowledge and helped me understand their views for the benefit of the whole child. In writing this book I have needed to deal with contradictions in their philosophies as well as with common ground, and I hope that my synthesis and condensation of their ideas, together with my own, will be of interest to them as well as to parents. The practical ideas and imagination of parents, families and people with disabilities have been an inspiration and of special value to me. Much more could have been included, but this book can only offer an approach which might serve as a foundation for many more ideas.

My style of working in a functional and integrated way may be familiar to some people. It seems to me inevitable if one is a keyworker with a child with one or more disabilities. The keyworker needs the back-up of a team of specialists in each condition that disables a child, so that practical suggestions can be made following the specialised diagnoses and assessments made by the whole team. Naturally the active participation of parents, families and children in a team assessment is essential.

Children with disabilities

Many different conditions may disable a child. However, what all these children have in common is that they grow and develop, and they can learn and actively participate according to their own ability. Any active participation by a child makes it easier to care for him.

All children must also be fed, washed, dressed, toileted and played with. They need to develop these skills as best they can, becoming as independent as possible. They all deserve our faith and encouragement, and I hope that the emotional and social aspects in both pictures and text will contribute to their growth in self-esteem.

Developmental stages

In this book the developmental stages are broad, selected abilities are emphasised and some of the sequences are modified according to the particular impairments. Experience tells us that development is highly individual when children have impairments, so that wide parameters are necessary.

The developmental 'ages' I have given tend to be in the 'late normal' range, since it is normal to be late when a child cannot see well and cannot move or understand as efficiently as other children. For example, a blind child or a child with cerebral palsy cannot appreciate where his body parts are and what they may be able to do. This delays moving. A blind child or a child with learning disabilities cannot easily understand that an object is still there even though he cannot see it. This delays his understanding of his world. Children with multiple disabilities may be frail and are likely to suffer from respiratory conditions, constipation or epilepsy. These and other health problems can also delay development. Children with disabilities tend to have frequent or long periods in hospital, and these, too, may slow their progress, as will the emotional stress that is likely in a family when a child has a disability.

Despite all these delays, progress is still possible and can be slow but sure. How far a child progresses will vary, and it is difficult to make an accurate forecast about his future as an adult. A 'normal' life of friends, family and interests, and possibly useful employment and marriage, should not be ruled out. Families, professionals and children who adopt a positive attitude can achieve exciting results.

Although parents and medical people have to bear in mind what is wrong with a child, this does not mean that his abilities should be forgotten, as may happen when parents are shocked or upset. Throughout the book I have concentrated on the child's developing abilities, and on what he or she has already achieved. My aim is to stress that *ability is a possibility*.

The main focus of the book is on the first two to three years of a child's life, since the abilities acquired then normally form the basis for all subsequent learning and most later skills.

About this book

The book is planned so that a carer (usually a parent) can select a daily life activity which he or she considers a priority. Particular ideas are therefore repeated in each of the chapters on daily activities, so that any chapter can be used without reference to the others. These repetitions not only help the child to learn better, but remind the carer to use essential ideas when teaching all the daily activities.

All the ideas apply equally to boys and girls. To make this clear, some chapters are written with 'he' and some with 'she', entirely at random. Carers may of course be either male or female, fathers or mothers.

PART ONE

BEFORE YOU START

1 THERAPY IN DAILY LIFE

In this book you will find numerous practical ideas from your child's therapy which have been brought together and fitted into everyday activities such as eating, washing and playing. In this way the whole child is being treated. Some people treat different parts of a child quite separately, but increasing numbers of parents and professionals now want ways of helping the whole child. Yet the methods for one part of a child may act against methods for another part. I have therefore selected methods which do work together in each activity.

In the same way, a number of parents of children with multiple disabilities have told me that experts in one disability sometimes contradict the advice of experts in another disability. I have selected methods on which there is general agreement. Many parents and children with disabilities have used the ideas in this book and found them valuable. So choose what suits you to improve your lives and give your children ideas for more development.

I hope that professional people will find the approach useful as a framework into which they can add their special knowledge and skills. Any professional who is a specialist in one disability will find practical suggestions for managing the other disabilities in a whole child.

GETTING ON WELL TOGETHER

When you feed, wash and dress your child, you share each other's pleasure in the activity. Of course, caring for any child has its ups and downs, and where additional problems exist there is likely to be some difficulty. Practical ideas are therefore very important, to make your everyday activities more enjoyable and easier for both you and your child. They will help your feelings of warm giving and receiving to grow, as well as your joy in your child's achievements, no matter how small.

Along with practical ideas you need the constant support and encouragement of your partner and other members of your family. Your friends and neighbours can also back you up. Sensitive help and encouragement from professional people enable your child to respond more positively to your handling of him or her. It is often valuable if you can find someone to whom you can talk and who also knows the problems that you will be dealing with.

WHAT MATTERS MOST?

Over many years of experience with children with disabilities and those who care for them, I have learnt that it is essential to follow their lead as to what is most relevant to their lives. They have guided me to work on such daily activities as feeding, washing, dressing, toileting, playing, helping their child get out of bed and move from place to place. As a therapist I thought it important to build 'therapy' into these daily activities, making it possible for a child to master his own symptoms as he strives to achieve what he can in his everyday life. The way these activities are carried out focuses on what you and your child know already, together with special ideas from therapists and teachers. In this way therapy can be functional and fun because it relates directly to everyday routines which also offer opportunities for playful interaction between you and your child.

Play is not only a part of child-caring activities but has its own special times of day for you and your child. Play merges into work as a young child develops and becomes older. Therefore everyday household routines, as well as later work activities, can be used as part of the approach presented in this book. It is relevant not only to children, but also to adolescents and adults with disabilities.

WHY WE USE DAILY LIVING ACTIVITIES

There are many advantages in using daily living activities. Let's take a look at them.

1 *A daily living activity consists of the following abilities, which every child needs:*
Controlling postures or balancing.
Moving.
Using hands.
Looking.
Listening.
Sensing: using touch, pressure, temperature, smell, taste, senses of movement and balance.
Understanding: what a child sees, hears and senses, what to do and how to do it.
Communicating with and without speech.

2 *Daily activities create interplay between all abilities*
During the process of learning a whole activity, any child is helped by the interplay between all his abilities which form the particular activity. For example, during dressing, when he uses his hands he will also use all his senses and control his balance. He comes to understand what he is doing and communicates it by showing you what he can do. Or when your child communicates her love for you in playful moments, she moves towards you, puts her arms around you, touches you and looks into your eyes. When a child is specially interested in one ability, such as looking, moving or tasting, he uses this in the context of a whole activity for which the ability is required.

3 *A child with multiple disabilities is rarely totally disabled*
There are a few children who are totally blind or completely paralysed, but even they can find ways of compensating for these impairments by developing their unimpaired abilities to their full potential. Even when a child has impairments, you need to remember that some ability may remain which we call 'residual ability'. So if your child has a severe visual impairment there may still be some *residual* vision. If your child has a hearing impairment or deafness, there may still be some *residual* hearing. If your child has a physical handicap, such as cerebral palsy, there may still be some *residual* movement or *residual* control of posture, or both. Finally, if your child has learning disabilities, he or she may still retain *some* understanding. All these remaining abilities have to be detected and can be further developed.

Besides these residual abilities your child may well have completely *unimpaired*

14

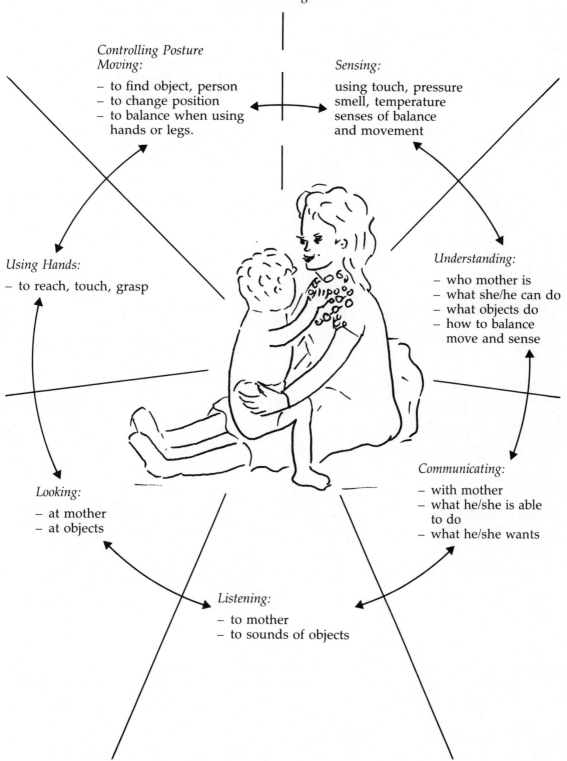

We Bring it All Together
as we are together

Controlling Posture Moving:

– to find object, person
– to change position
– to balance when using hands or legs.

Sensing:

using touch, pressure
smell, temperature
senses of balance
and movement

Using Hands:

– to reach, touch, grasp

Understanding:

– who mother is
– what she/he can do
– what objects do
– how to balance
  move and sense

Looking:

– at mother
– at objects

Communicating:

– with mother
– what he/she is able
  to do
– what he/she wants

Listening:

– to mother
– to sounds of objects

15

abilities. A child who is blind and has cerebral palsy may hear well and retain other senses. He may also have normal understanding. A deaf-blind child may nevertheless move, balance and sense well, and a child who is blind and has learning disabilities may be able to move. These unimpaired abilities also need detection and further development.

We are already aware that unimpaired abilities can interact with one another in a daily activity. The residual abilities can also interact so that they can develop to their optimum levels.

4 *Physical disabilities can be treated within daily activities*

This is possible provided the correct guidance and opportunities are given to your child. As he focuses on acquiring abilities, he must at the same time master whatever physical disabilities he may have. These disabilities are then decreased and in some cases can be eliminated. In other words, the 'therapeutic exercise' is incorporated into the way in which a child learns a daily activity. These are some physical disabilities that can be improved:

Spasticity or other muscle stiffness decreases as a child is correctly positioned and encouraged to move correctly. These correcting positions, combining a change of position with correct ways of moving, can be directly involved with the achievement of the daily tasks.

Involuntary movements, tremors or spasms are best controlled when a child carries out purposeful movements. These can be the actions used for carrying out a daily activity.

Weakness decreases when muscles are used repeatedly, so regularly exercising them while performing daily activities helps to strengthen them. Particularly weak muscles need extra attention while they are being used for daily tasks. If, say, the bending muscles of a knee are weak, then repeating bending actions during washing, dressing or playing will improve their performance.

Deformities may be prevented, decreased or overcome by corrective positions, changes of position and corrective movements. When spasticity or weakness are minimised then deformities are minimised. Once again the selection of appropriate positions and corrective movements to carry out daily tasks can at the same time largely deal with deformities.

Abnormal reflexes which individual children have when there is slow development or damage to the brain can also be overcome, or reduced, when the children are helped to develop control of their heads and bodies as they balance and move. In this book I have suggested postures and movements which control most abnormal reflexes.

Poor balance and co-ordination. A child with full abilities increases his balance and co-ordination of his body and eye–hand co-ordination as he develops daily skills at different stages. Such improvement is also used for a child with disabilities. The practical ideas to do this are selected according to each child's levels of balance and co-ordination.

5 *Daily activities have more meaning for children*

Children can see more meaning in methods which obviously help them achieve part or all of a daily activity. Even when specialised treatments are also needed, these should be explained in terms of what they contribute to the child's wishes or interests.

Daily activities are more familiar, take place in the well-known surroundings of home or school and lead to the child's growing independence, which in turn will motivate him to continue making efforts to improve. We are all motivated to learn what has meaning for us, especially if we have chosen to do it!

6   Brothers, sisters and other family members can participate

When therapy methods can be incorporated into what family members already know about children, then they can help out and so feel involved and appreciated. Extra help by all family members relieves the pressures on the parents, especially the mother. The parents may then have more energy to devote to each other and to the rest of the family.

7   Time is saved

When therapy becomes part of what has to be done anyway, then time is saved for both family and professionals, including time spent travelling for extra therapy. Repetition of therapy ideas at home is more likely to happen if the therapy has meaning in a family's lifestyle, so the more a child does the better he gets. As a result, less time has to be allocated for physiotherapy, occupational therapy, speech therapy or teaching sessions.

However, you must allow time to learn how best to do the daily activities. Each one of us learns at our own pace. As your child begins to help, more time becomes available for parents, carers and professionals. This, together with the time-saving already mentioned, shows why daily living training is so important.

8   Different professionals can collaborate better

Parents may feel that they receive contradictory advice, as well as having to practise many separate home treatments suggested by different professionals. It is possible for professionals to pool their ideas for helping a child learn each daily living activity and so obtain more co-ordination of his programme. Better teamwork is promoted between professionals, parents and carers.

Parents find it helpful if one keyworker brings together all the ideas of the team who know their child. Relating to one person or keyworker can be easier for both parent and child. It is important to see this keyworker often and work together in a developing relationship of trust.

9   Confidence grows sooner

During daily living activities children's participation, no matter how small, creates positive feelings in them. Those feelings build self-esteem in the children as they
   —feel some control of their function
   —feel of some help to those they love
   —feel some responsibility.
Parents and carers also find their confidence growing as they discover how much they

can help their children, have more control in their children's habilitation programmes and share responsibility with professionals.

When we work with babies and children so that they take some responsibility, control or active participation, they often develop that self-esteem which leads to their own inventiveness. They find their own solutions for their tasks of everyday living. Therefore if progress is not always possible in all abilities, the person with disabilities could discover individual solutions. Confident parents and carers also find imaginative solutions to carrying out daily activities. However, we must always be open to what children themselves can devise to pursue their interests and solve problems of daily living.

Specialised treatments and special teaching sessions may still be necessary

These will be needed depending on each child's particular condition and its severity. These treatments and teaching sessions complement the daily life activities, but cannot replace them. It is important to realise that, although abilities can increase with special training, not all physical and mental disabilities or impairments can be cured. Nevertheless, the physical disabilities and other problems can be mastered to a greater or lesser degree.

WALKING, TALKING AND THINKING

These are the main achievements we hope to develop in our children. They are the functions most obviously affected when a child has multiple handicaps. The basic abilities leading to walking, talking and thinking are also the basic abilities for daily activities.

Walking

Walking depends upon postural control (balancing), moving and using hands for initial support. Catching sight of something that interests him, or hearing or smelling it, encourages a child's walking to develop. Understanding why and how to walk as well as remembering the way to do it are also important.

Talking

Speech develops after children learn the meanings of words and phrases. This knowledge comes from the exploration they make of their environment, which in turn depends on using postural control, movement, hands, sight, senses, hearing and understanding. Hearing and understanding are particularly important. Once speech itself develops this helps the progress of all the other abilities.

Thinking

For thinking, a child needs all the basic abilities which are used for developing walking and talking. Each learning experience gained during balancing, moving, using

18

hands, hearing and sensing helps him develop understanding and so progress in thinking.

Progress in all the abilities therefore results not only in improvements in self-care and play but simultaneously develops walking, talking and thinking.

Rate of progress

It is in the first two to three years that all the basic abilities for walking, talking and thinking are normally being developed. These are the foundations for later abilities and contribute to more refined and additional skills in later childhood. A child with one or more disabilities will need longer than two to three years to achieve the basic abilities.

Once these abilities are achieved by an able young child, it still takes years before he can carry out the complete range of daily activities well and independently. Normally a child takes five to six years to learn to dress alone, and about six years to eat alone with a fork and knife or to bathe completely alone. Naturally, it will take still longer for a child with multiple disabilities to achieve the same independence. Training will have to continue into adolescence and sometimes adulthood.

Nevertheless, parents will continue to observe slow but sure progress at their child's own rate of development. Each ability should be broken down into smaller stages so that progress can be achieved and noted. There is no 'age' when development can be said to stop. All of us continue to learn new skills, whether we are able-bodied or not.

2 HOW TO DO THE ACTIVITIES

As a parent and carer you are going to bring up your child as you would any other. After all, a child with disabilities is still a child, with the same needs for love and security. You know your child as a person and that will affect your decisions about how to use the special suggestions in this book. You may know some of these ideas already or want to change or leave out others, for each child has an individual personality and different abilities and disabilities. Having read through the techniques proposed, take them as useful examples. You can then work out your own methods to suit you, your family and your child. No single book can have ideas all of which will suit every child and so cannot guarantee results for all children. It would be wise to look at the book with your therapist and teacher so that they can demonstrate activities when you feel unsure and also add their own ideas according to what they know of your child and you.

When you are planning how you will do the activities it helps if you ask some basic questions which are briefly discussed in this chapter:

1 Which daily activity is my goal?
2 Which daily activity interests or might arouse interest in my child?
3 What abilities do we need for each daily activity?
4 What are my child's present abilities?
5 Which abilities does my child still need to learn?
6 How do we develop my child's abilities and help him learn them?
7 How are we progressing?

QUESTIONS 1 AND 2: SELECT AN ACTIVITY

Start with an activity which presents problems for you. This might be feeding, dressing or washing. It might simply be something that you would like to do better. Also, select an activity that interests or might interest your child—it may be the same one or another. Once training begins and your child realises he can do something, his interest will grow. Some children do not know what interests them or what they want to do; they also find it difficult to tell you what they want. Besides watching your child during activities, give him the chance to experience what it is like to make his own choices. For example, start by giving him practice in making small choices such as indicating which he likes in his bowl, which shoe he wants you to put on first and which arm you should dry first. Let him take a moment to choose between two toys or two play activities. After a time he may well choose a daily activity.

You need only take on training as many daily activities as you feel able to cope with. Expect other family members to help and support you. Perhaps they would like to train your child in a different activity. Other carers, therapists and teachers will help you on home visits or at your child's nursery, centre or school. You may meet a health visitor or nurse who helps you with ordinary child care activities and can provide additional ideas related to your child's special difficulties.

QUESTIONS 3, 4, AND 5: STAGES OF DEVELOPMENT

As I said in the last chapter, each daily activity is made up of abilities such as controlling posture, looking, understanding and so on. In children these abilities develop from basic to more advanced stages. For example, a baby's ability to move or use his eyes would be at a more basic stage than that of an older child. When a child has difficulties it is advisable to begin training at the basic stages of child development and progress to the more advanced ones. You and your child will generally follow normal developmental stages, and you and your professional advisers will adjust these to suit your child's individual problems. In Chapter 4, the Developmental Framework will guide you in finding what your child can do and what he or she still needs to achieve.

At the various stages your child will have his own abilities and will find it easier to achieve some activities than others. By watching him, you will see that some abilities are just beginning, some are rarely used and that he can carry out some slowly or in a laboured way. By observing ALL the abilities at each stage of the daily activity you will certainly find something your child can do, despite his multiple impairments. You will also discover which abilities he still needs to learn.

QUESTION 6: HOW TO DEVELOP THE ABILITIES

a *Work at your child's developmental stages—and just beyond them*
To give your child confidence, start with what he *can* do. He will then be more willing to practise those abilities which are unsteady, rarely used, laboured or carried out very slowly. Then, finally, challenge him with opportunities for new abilities. Try to train them at stages just beyond your child's current abilities so that he has to try hard to achieve them. Do not expect him to practise activities that are too far ahead of him, or too easy.

b *The way in which a child does what he can varies*
These various ways may be 'normal' in the context of your child's specific impairments. For example, he may go through a longer period of using mouthing for exploring things if his hands are severely affected or if his vision is severely impaired. He may use an unusual tilt of the head to see better, or he may hold his head down to listen better if he cannot see. You only need to correct unusual ways of doing actions if these might block his further development. Advice is included with the practical suggestions in this book and more should be obtained from your advisers and from other parents and people with disabilities.

c *Position your child so that he can function at his best*
This is the position in which he can begin to balance himself, move his limbs more easily, see and hear best and in which he is most comfortable. Ask the therapist about suitable equipment to support your child for such positions, but meanwhile train him to develop further control of his position so that in time he can 'outgrow' the equipment.

d *Change your child's positions*
Once your child is just achieving an ability reliably, practise this ability in another position. If he has been lying down, try it with him in a sitting position or standing

supported. Changing his position offers many different opportunities for him to develop posture control, movement, use of hands, looking, listening and using senses. He gains more understanding of all these aspects when he learns them in different positions. Encourage your child actively to change his own positions or to participate as much as he can to help you change his positions.

If a child remains in any one position for a long period of time he may feel uncomfortable. Later, when he is older, he may even feel pain in some of these postures. In each of the different positions you also need to look at how he holds his head, body and limbs. The posture of each part of his body, head, arms and legs should not be the same for most of the day.

e   *Prevent and correct abnormal postures*
If a child has abnormal postures and they become a habit, it will lead to fixed deformities called contractures. Abnormal postures might block further development of abilities. You therefore need to correct the lying, sitting, kneeling and standing postures as much as you can, as well as to change them as often as possible.

Correct postures are given in each chapter on the daily activities.

f   *Corrective movements are used for daily activities*
Here are some general suggestions to help you:

—Encourage your child to stretch out his arms or legs, body or head if he usually bends them during actions.
—Encourage him to bend his arms and legs, body and head if he usually overstretches, arches or stretches them during actions.
—Encourage him to move his arms and legs away from his body if they are usually held or moved close to his body.
—Encourage him to move his hands, arms and legs towards his body if they are usually held or moved out sideways and away from his body.
—Encourage him to use both sides of his body, both arms and both legs, at the same time. Also encourage the use of one side after another when a child usually uses one side of his body only. Keep your child interested in having his head and body in the centre if he usually prefers one side.

All these corrective actions are included in the suggestions for daily activities and the development of all the abilities. Your physiotherapist can advise you on your child's individual needs.

How to help a child learn the abilities

a   *One person should help a child* most or all of the time at first. This is often his mother with whom his most significant relationship is being developed. Once he has more confidence and more ability he will be able to accept another carer, and as time goes by more people will be accepted. The way one person handles a child is more predictable and consistent, making it easier for him to feel secure and to learn to anticipate what will happen. We all feel more secure in a strange world if we know what will happen next.

22

Some common patterns of postures and movements which need correcting if a child uses them frequently.

b *Use teaching and therapy methods which suit your child and you.* A few methods which suit many people are given in this book. They are a starting point. Use what works for you and find your own ideas in time. Always search for what your child, you and your family enjoy.

This does not mean that your child only does what is easy for him, but that through interesting, enjoyable ideas he works at obtaining posture control, movement, looking, listening, sensing and understanding.

c *Use small steps* in teaching any ability so that it will be easier for the child to learn *and* easier for you to see how well you are progressing. This book has developmental stages, but you may have to make still smaller steps within these stages.

d *Guide your child if necessary.* We physically guide a child's actions and give him support in his postures so that he understands what he has to do in order to do a task. Repeat this guidance and make it clear. To do this you may sometimes guide firmly, over and over again so that your child's attention is focused on these actions and on what they might achieve. Be aware of when he begins to take over these actions or part of them, as you can then gradually remove your guidance. Also release your hold on him as he takes over the balance or control of his posture.

Usually you should begin a task and then give your child the satisfaction of finishing it alone. Once your physical guidance is no longer needed, you can just use words or short phrases to guide his actions. Give him an encouraging word to signal that he should do a task or continue doing it once he knows what to do.

DO NOT ALWAYS GUIDE your child. There will be abilities he can develop on his own. Give him time to attempt a new ability independently, or to take over completely from you once you have shown him what to do. Give him time to solve problems in his own way, which may be unusual but not 'wrong'. Allow him to make mistakes, too, and learn how to correct himself. Each child will differ in the amount of guidance he needs, how much you can allow him to struggle a bit on his own and how much you should combine both of these approaches.

e *Reward your child's efforts.* Having a child work at his own developmental stages and just beyond them allows him to achieve something for himself. Your child's own satisfaction in achievement is his reward and is most important if he is to feel his own control and find his own understanding. Only when a child with very severe disabilities cannot understand that his small achievement is worthwhile, or that just trying to do anything is valuable, even though full achievement is not yet apparent, are your rewards needed. They should be given *immediately* after he has done what he can.

Reward the child with much praise, claps, hugs, stroking, physical rewards such as food, vibrating toys, music or other pleasures. Such rewards for 'trying' encourage him to continue working. However, take care that you don't overdo them. A child who is trying because he wants to will only need to know that you are pleased with him.

Show him your appreciation by a touch, by your quiet, encouraging attention or by smiling in approval. Tell him what he did well so that he learns what is expected of him – for example, 'You stretched out your arm nicely!' or, 'You took off your sock well!' He will understand your tone of voice and your smile, if not all the words. If he fails to do anything, ignore this and say calmly, 'We'll try again,' or, 'Have a rest now.'

f *Focus your child's attention* on one difficult ability at a time, but make sure he uses those that he has already acquired at the same time. Try incorporating additional abilities which need more practice. However, avoid distracting him as you do this; don't bombard him with too many different things which interfere with learning and might upset him.

Keep checking that he is concentrating on what he is doing. To help him, the sessions may have to be short, or you may have to work in a quieter room. Always switch off the radio and television and remove distracting pictures. Perhaps shine a light on what he is working on. Give him your undivided attention when teaching him something he finds difficult. Remember to change positions only after he has achieved, or almost achieved, an ability in one position.

g *Give your child time* for sensing and accepting a new posture or movement, for using his hands, for looking and listening. Give him time to become aware of these abilities and so come to understand what is happening. He needs time to repeat the practical ideas over and over again. Above all, you must give him time to find his own way of solving any problems.

QUESTION 7: HOW ARE WE PROGRESSING?

As you carry out an activity, observe what your child can do and make a note, take a photograph or make a video recording. As time goes on and you and your child achieve more abilities, keep recording in the same way. You may use the headings of this book—Posture, Moving, Using Hands, Looking, Listening, Sensing, Communicating and Understanding—to guide your observations. Your therapists will have their own ways of helping you assess your child's progress.

If progress is too slow or there is none at all, break down the abilities into smaller steps so that you can see that there *is* progress, no matter how small. Be ready to use your common sense, imagination and knowledge as a parent to find other ways of solving the problems.

No one is perfect! Children still make progress if you simply do the best you can to be a 'good enough' parent. If you become anxious and tired you cannot help your child so well. Share the work with others and remember that some days will be better than others. Building up your child's self-esteem means that he, too, will gradually help.

3 COMMUNICATION

Although multiple disabilities make it more difficult to get through to your child, it is well known that if you take the time and trouble to establish a close personal relationship with him, you will succeed. In this way mothers of children with severe disabilities have developed extraordinary skills in communicating with them. Carers and professionals depend on a mother showing them how she can tell what her child likes and wants; what he dislikes and refuses to do; and how to convey to her child what he is expected to do. They are then better able to draw upon their special experience for each individual child and share their observations of the child as they get to know him.

The Daily Activities

While helping your child develop the various abilities within the daily activities, try to communicate to him as clearly and as simply as possible. You need to observe his responses so that you can adjust what you are showing him and how you are guiding him. Some ideas were given in Chapter 2, and you will find more under all the headings of the abilities, as well as under the heading 'Communicating' in each of the chapters on daily living activities.

YOUR COMMUNICATION

You communicate to your child:
- What his capacities are.
- What you expect from him.

You are helping him recognise that:
- He has sensations and movements, no matter how minimal.
- He can come to understand people and things through his senses of vision, hearing, touch, smell and taste, using his hands, moving and controlling his posture.
- It is both pleasurable and interesting to become aware of his senses, movements and postural control, and to obtain meaning with them.

You can show what more is expected of him in various ways:
- Sometimes you set the scene, create situations or provide various opportunities in which he can find his own ways of achieving abilities. Your way of communicating is then to give quiet attention, without any physical help, so that he feels your confidence in him as he tries to achieve an ability as best he can.
- Sometimes you need to guide him physically, support him or use a technical aid or special position so that he learns what to do and can make active efforts.
- Sometimes you remove guidance gradually, waiting for his own action. This communicates to him that he should take over more and more. By trying this you discover his abilities.
- Sometimes he progresses so that he understands your guidance when it is given in gestures, signs, words, simple phrases and finally in simple instructions. Naturally, you should avoid talking too much as this will distract him from concentrating on what he is doing.

In these various ways your child's understanding increases as he begins to make sense of your communications. At the same time he is developing more responsibility himself, especially by having many opportunities to function on his own. Your communication then is that you share his pleasure!

YOUR CHILD'S COMMUNICATION

You need to recognise and respond warmly to any indication that your child is making contact with you. Look carefully for any smile, cry, body wriggle, slight tension or even small movements of his fingers or toes or opening of his mouth. Your response will encourage him to continue to communicate in these ways. He will then try to make you understand him further.

However, because of his disabilities he may use unusual ways of receiving or giving messages to you. For example, he may drop his head down more, become very still with an expressionless face, smile too much, frown excessively or repeat words and phrases without apparent meaning except that this is a way of making contact. He may use his physical symptoms and over-arch, twist, thrust, increase his tremors and involuntary movements and grimace excessively. All this may look as if he is withdrawing from you, when in fact he may be telling you of his delight and excitement and concentrating hard on what you are saying or doing with him. You must recognise that he *is* communicating, and respond to him. Your alertness to his communications makes him more willing to learn the socially acceptable ways of indicating his wishes.

Your child may also still be using baby ways of letting you know what he wants. For example, he screams, increases his breathing, kicks, coughs, bites or throws things. Once again, you need to teach him more acceptable and therefore more developmentally appropriate ways of communicating.

Whenever your child uses unusual or unacceptable ways of communicating you can help him develop in the following way. You respond to his communication by giving him what he wants or likes *if* he uses acceptable indications, such as a nod, a shake of the head, a turn to what he wants, a natural gesture indicating wanting to eat, sleep or drink; or if he uses other gestures such as holding out both arms to be picked up, putting out an arm for dressing or opening his mouth for food. You may have to guide him physically to carry out any of these actions, and then give him what he wants.

There are communications which depend on seeing and using particular body movements such as pointing with one finger, turning to look at whoever is talking or waving goodbye to someone. In view of your child's specific problems, he cannot be expected to develop such communications until much later than usual.

He may also develop communications or gestures which are not perfectly co-ordinated actions but which do still convey his meaning. You can teach him such actions, but they will also occur spontaneously if your child feels you are interested in his point of view.

Using imitation to show him what to do is difficult since it depends on sight and understanding. You cannot easily communicate by 'pretend' games either, as these also depend on him seeing you, the objects and the surroundings. In time, imitating sounds and movements and pretending in play develop, although later than they do

27

in children who have no disabilities. Children with multiple disabilities will eventually manage all this in their own way or by using their own imagination.

Some children have special problems with talking and understanding speech and other ways of communicating. Ask a speech therapist for extra help and specialised treatment if your child has problems like these.

UNCO-OPERATIVE CHILDREN

Some children use baby communication or a variety of strange communications to say they refuse to do something, or they withdraw, becoming passive. They may communicate fear, anxiety and their feelings of being over-pressurised to do something. Once again, you should teach abilities well within your child's developmental level, to reassure him, and progress more slowly at his pace to try abilities just beyond his developmental stage. Make sure that your guidance is simple and clear to him and that he finds it enjoyable and interesting to do what you expect of him. You may have to persuade or coax him so that he gets a taste of success in abilities which he is reluctant to try.

These and various other behavioural difficulties are very individual and you should discuss them with the professionals who are advising you. They can plan ways of helping to suit a particular child's needs. Nevertheless, any development of his abilities gives *any* child more confidence and the courage to do things which he formerly refused in anger, frustration or fear of failure.

Learning to Make a Choice

Whenever possible, encourage your child to make a choice either by looking at what he wants, making a gesture or later speaking, if that develops. Respond to him after giving him time to show what he wants. He will then learn that it is worthwhile trying to communicate. So do not be too kind by anticipating *all* his wants. He will also become more co-operative if his choices are respected.

UNDERSTANDING AND EXPRESSING COMMUNICATION

Because of the extra problems which children face when they have multiple disabilities, they need more time to gain the everyday experiences of able-bodied children. It takes time before *any* child, able-bodied or not, can understand these experiences. This understanding is necessary before speech can develop as a means of expression. Meanwhile, as I have said, any expression by your child, with or without speech, should be encouraged. Such expression also develops his process of learning and his speech.

Non-Speech Communication

Besides expressing himself through sounds, body actions and gestures, your child may be taught to use specialised signing systems, special devices or computers. Your professional advisers will be able to tell when your child is ready and interested to attempt such tasks, and which system he will be able to use.

RELATING TO CHILDREN

We all know how important communication is to any child in order to:
- Indicate his wants, thoughts and feelings
- Control events in his environment
- Make some decisions
- Grow in self-confidence as a result
- Interact better socially.

Although you should always respond to your child's communications as much as possible, you must also remember that you want to encourage his development—clearly, a child who gets his own way all the time will block his own development. Respect his view, but modify it if necessary, to make him more willing to accept what you want of him, and share decisions with him. You may also have to avoid his smiling or talking if he uses this to distract himself from trying a difficult activity. Above all, remember that any communication depends fundamentally on establishing a warm bond with your child.

IMOGEN

Imogen likes looking at strips of silver paper hanging near her, but soon loses interest. Looking at the silver paper with her mother increases her pleasure, and her mother also shakes or waves the paper, or changes Imogen's position, so that more interesting effects are created.

By accident Imogen feels the paper touching her leg and automatically kicks it away. This creates even more interest—and perhaps a little fear. Her mother reassures her and even shows her how to do it again, but should leave Imogen to decide whether to do so herself. It is fun to become aware of looking at something. It is interesting to become aware that you yourself can make something happen. Later, Imogen may also understand that if paper is kicked it reacts one way—but if her brother is kicked he behaves quite differently!

Her mother also gives Imogen the silver paper and encourages her to return it to her in a playful game. This giving and taking develops communication so that Imogen makes a sound or hand movement when it is her turn to take the paper. Taking turns to make sounds to each other further develops the contact between Imogen and her mother.

PART TWO

DAILY ACTIVITIES

4 THE DEVELOPMENTAL FRAMEWORK

The developmental framework on pages 34 and 35 may be used in five ways:

1 *The framework shows you the main abilities you are aiming to develop* in the first, second, third and fourth stages of any daily activity. The earlier, and sometimes easier, abilities are given in the first stages, progressing to the more difficult and more advanced abilities in the second, third and fourth stages. The abilities are arranged in the order that many children develop them. In the framework you will see drawings for reference, of a child demonstrating various abilities. In the remaining chapters of the book complete drawings are given, showing you how to help your own child achieve these abilities.

2 *The framework can be used to observe your child* because it highlights abilities to try with him or her. Using the practical suggestions in each stage, and your own knowledge of your child, you can find what he or she can do and what he or she still needs to learn to do.

3 *The framework gives ideas on what to do next.* Once you get to know what your child can do you discover which abilities are advanced and which are less advanced. Concentrate on the primary ability which is less advanced but also use ideas under all headings of the other abilities as there is so much interaction between all abilities.
   Try the item just beyond what your child can do well *and* beyond what he or she is just beginning to do. Practise what he or she can only do in an unsure, slow, occasional manner. Train the next item which is new to your child.

4 *The framework shows what a child has omitted* in his or her development. Progress of more advanced abilities can sometimes continue without a particular earlier ability. It is important to discuss this with your therapist or teacher, as in individual children some earlier abilities are essential for future progress.

5 *The framework can be used for observing general progress.* Over many months you will see how your child progresses to more items in each stage, and then on to later stages. However, to see progress sooner, break down each ability or item into smaller steps.

Remember:
- Children are individual.
- The developmental framework outlines main abilities, items or skills. You and your child will discover others. Your therapist and other professionals will suggest more for your particular child.
- Under each heading—Controlling Posture, Moving, Using Hands, Looking, Listening, Sensing, Communicating and Understanding—there are ideas which may well appear under any of the other headings. This is because there is so much interaction between all abilities.
- There is an overlap between the last part of one stage and the beginning of the next stage.

	FIRST STAGES		SECOND STAGES		
CONTROLLING POSTURE, MOVING					
Lying on side	Head centre, hands together	Rolls to side	Leans on elbow	Reaches and grasps feet	Comes up to sitting, leans on elbow, then leaning on hands
Lying on stomach	Raises head on elbows / Reaches out / On hands / Rolls over		Creeping / On hands and knees. Crawling / Comes up to kneel supported. Knee-walking supported		
Lying on back	Head centre hands together / Raises head and coming up to sit with help / Raises hips with help		Rolling over. Rolls continuously / Raises hips on own / Pulls self to sit, holding on		
Sitting	Fully supported / Less support, head control / Leans on hands / Leans against table and holds on/ grasps		Sits alone. Begins to bottom-shuffle with help / Sits and reaches in all directions / Catches balance on hand if tipped / Pulls self up to standing holding on		
Standing	Fully supported / Well supported, grasps bar or leans on hands. Head control / NO stepping now		Stands grasping supports, less help / Leans on hands or holds on as moves one foot or uses one hand / May step with much support		
USING HANDS	Open hands / Hands together / Grasps if placed in hands / Hand to mouth. Reaches out		Hand to mouth with object, spoon, biscuit / Fingers used	Reaches and grasps feet, body, toy. Picks up with whole hand / Uses both hands. Transfers hand to hand	Lets go into container
LOOKING	Awareness of own vision. Watches mother's face. Nearby vision. Follows face/objects. Looks at own hands, body		Looks and reaches nearby, in all directions near front. Sees smaller objects. Watches moving people and farther away		
LISTENING	Awareness of own hearing. Responds to mother's voice. Gentle sounds. Increasing interest in sounds		Turns to voices with eyes, head, near front. Reaches for sounds within sight. Listens more attentively. Associates sounds with everyday events		
SENSING	Awareness of touch, smell, taste and of movement of posture grows. Enjoys friendly handling		More attentive to all senses. Looks to where touched, smell is		
COMMUNICATING	Gets to know mother/carer. Begins to interact. Smiles, cries, uses body communication—nuzzles. Makes sounds		Prefers own carer. Makes sounds, body actions, to communicate specific wants. Babbles more. Begins taking turns to interact. Recognises more people. Understands words in specific situations		
UNDERSTANDING	Recognises mother/carer and own bottle. Pats carer, bottle and toy. Takes breast/bottle to mouth		Recognises mealtimes, bathtimes, sounds of known people. Chewing. Feeds self with biscuit. Drinks with help. Finger feeds. Puts out limb for dressing. Begins to look for partly covered objects. Anticipates routines		

Changes postures with less or no support

Bottom-shuffles down stairs and along floor

Crawls up and down stairs; slides down stairs

Tilting and saving self from falling with arms/leg

Stands alone. Stands and lifts up arms

Stands on one foot with help

Steps, cruises sideways

Stairs. Going up is easier

Stairs. Less help going down and up

Steps with help

Walks alone

Walks carrying object

Runs, jumps, hops with guidance

Body actions with more use of space, direction and speed. Inside, above, underneath, along and behind large objects when moves

Places, fetches objects from floor without falling

Rides tricycles and playthings

Climbs onto chair and furniture

Walks backwards, steps over objects, between objects, over different surfaces

Pincer grasps. Picks up

Pulls and pushes

Places and lets go of smaller objects into smaller containers

Grasps tool and bangs

Rolls, throws (kicks) balls

More precise grasps and manipulation

Screw-toys

Lids

Post box toys

Simple, large peg-boards

Threads beads, rings on sticks. PUZZLES

Tears, crumples paper

Objects farther away; above, below, at side and then behind. Reaches out and moves to find sounds or objects. Finds smaller objects, softer sounds

Making sounds, music

Catches balls smaller size

Picks up tiny objects if sees them (or feels for them)

Enjoys pets, their sounds, movement and smells

Water play

More use of hands, movement, taste, smell, touch to understand

Sorting different objects—more complicated tasks. Hand activities include sensing

Responds to name. Understands simple instructions and some words with gesture. Uses more gestures. Speech develops and is very individual. Taking turns in making sounds and giving you an object

Speech is individual in development. May give own name. Talks about sorting, matching activities and all other learning. Enjoys moving to songs more; naming body parts alone

Sorts objects, clothes, cutlery. Pairs and matches textures, smells, sounds, tastes, sizes, shapes and colours according to child's abilities. Looks for object, person out of sight or out of hearing. Sequences of daily activities interest child more. Finger feeds, places food into mouth more precisely. Holds cup

Sequences of daily activities longer, more understood. *Eating:* Uses spoon alone, fork and begins to use knife and fork. Drinks alone. *Dressing:* Takes off most clothes if unfastened, begins unfastening laces, buttons. *Washing:* Does hands alone. Helps more. *Toileting:* Success varies in day. Dry nights

INTRODUCTION TO THE PRACTICAL CHAPTERS
(*Chapters 5, 6, 7, 8, 9 and 10*)

The practical chapters on eating and drinking, washing, dressing, toileting, playing and moving from place to place add to your own ideas on finding the best ways to carry out these daily activities. The chapters offer you:

Suggested Positions
These minimise the physical symptoms of most children so that you can manage the activities more easily. At the same time, such positions enable your child gradually to develop abilities.

Suggested Abilities
These are controlling posture and moving, using hands, looking, listening, sensing, communicating and understanding. These headings appear as captions throughout these chapters.

Suggested Stages of Development
The abilities are given in easier to more difficult developmental stages. These stages are based approximately on the normal developmental stages:

  First stages: 0–6 months.
  Second stages: 6–12 months.
  Third stages: 1–2 years.
  Fourth stages: 2–3 years.

Suggested practical ideas and hints are given for the abilities and their developmental stages. However, remember that you will see practical suggestions under one caption which could well appear under one or more of the other captions. This is because all aspects of a child are interconnected.

The captions to the different abilities may appear one after another in this book, but in real life these various abilities are happening at the same time. When you help with one ability you are helping with others simultaneously, as I explained in Chapters 2 and 3.

How to Use the Chapters on the Daily Activities

First look at the pictures in the chapter on the daily living activity you have selected. Plan to use about three positions which you and your child can manage. These should be chosen from:

Child lying on her side.
Child lying on her stomach.
Child lying on her back.
Sitting position.
Standing position.

- Use at least one position with your child upright, as the upright position is best for her when she is using her eyes, ears and balance (posture control).

- Use different positions for different aspects of a daily activity. For example, wash with your child lying on her sides, dry with her lying on her stomach and have her sitting for washing hands and face. Another example might be dressing top clothes in a sitting position, trousers or skirt in a lying position and managing socks and shoes in a kneeling position on one knee with the other knee and foot held in front.
- The positions you have not chosen for one particular daily activity may be used for another.
- Now look at the caption for Controlling Posture and Moving opposite the picture. You will have learnt at which developmental stage your child manages any position from Chapter 4. You will now be able to see these postures and movements in the context of the particular daily activity you and your child have selected.
- The other captions, under Using Hands, Looking, Listening, Sensing, Communicating and Understanding, relate to *any* position you have chosen for the daily activities. Once again, you will learn at which developmental stage your child may manage the other abilities by referring to Chapter 4. You will now be able to develop these abilities with the practical suggestions given under these captions.
- When your child needs to concentrate on more advanced postures and moving, use easier stages of the other abilities. However, when she is trying more difficult stages of other activities, keep her posture stable and comfortable. Always give time for this to happen.
- Start with what your child manages easily and try more difficult stages of all abilities after a time, in a few days, months or longer.

Special Recommendations

POSTURE CONTROL AND MOVING

Placing a child in position may take time if there is much stiffness in her body or if she is prone to excessive involuntary wriggling actions. This improves with practice. Give her time to accept new postures. Before beginning an activity she needs time to control any spasms, startles or involuntary movements. Move stiff children often and slowly.

USING HANDS

When guiding a child to touch and explore something, remember that *your touch* on her arm or hand should not distract her from attending to what she is exploring. This is not always possible if her hands are severely affected, for your physical guidance is then essential. In that case you can help her to touch and explore using other parts of her body and other senses. Meanwhile, do continue training her to use her hands.

LOOKING AND LISTENING

Make sure that your face and hands are in a good light when you are communicating what you expect your child to do, and when you talk and socialise with her. A good light on her body and hands also helps her watch what is happening during the activities. However, avoid dazzling her with a bright light.

Use noises and voices that will not startle her. Speak clearly and do not shout.

Instead, come close to her ear if she does not hear very well. Keep your voice pleasant and vary your tone.

SENSING
Use smells and other sensations that are genuinely helpful to your child. For example, a floral smell sprayed in the toilet or flower-scented soaps can be confusing for her if there are no flowers present.

UNDERSTANDING AND COMMUNICATING
Keep distractions to a minimum when she is concentrating. Give her your full attention when you are teaching anything new or difficult as part of an activity. Always let her know you have approached her, perhaps giving your name and greeting her by name. Let her know when you start an activity, when you stop, and when you change to another.

Keep to a routine as far as possible in daily activities. Follow the same sequence each time so that your child can learn to anticipate, co-operate and, eventually, initiate the activity herself and, one hopes, take it over after a time.

TOYS, FURNITURE AND EQUIPMENT
These are improving as time goes on and your therapists and teachers will let you know what is available to suit your own child.

Large playthings should be solid and stable.

Playthings and equipment with springs and bouncers may cause increased stiffness, spasms and involuntary movements. For example, a trampoline or a 'baby bouncer' may not suit your child. Careful supervision is needed with such equipment to ensure that it is safe and beneficial.

Rocking chairs and rocking toys also need supervision so that your child interacts with you rather than withdrawing into a rocking motion.

Fragile toys and small toys may be tasted and chewed and are not safe. Avoid sharp edges and parts that break off a toy or equipment.

Avoid leaving toys or objects where a child may trip over them. Always keep toys and furniture in the same place so that your child knows where they are. Show her their positions so that she uses them as 'landmarks' once she understands this. Later, furniture can be rearranged and toys and equipment put in different places. Show this new arrangement to your child as her understanding grows. If she has very poor sight, find ways of helping her to use tactile clues that she can understand, so that she knows where she is.

The Special Relationship between You and Your Child

As I said in Chapters 2 and 3, this relationship is crucial for helping your child develop. So use your ways of sharing affection and building a warm, trusting relationship with her. You may hold each other close, hug, cuddle, touch and squeeze each other. On your lap tilt, rock or move together in any position. Use rhythmic chants, songs and rhymes and talk to each other. Remember to go more slowly with your child if she is easily upset and dislikes being touched or moved. At some stages children may fall easily if tilted and are fearful of any change of position, so gentle handling is best.

Massage can be a way of making pleasant contact, but should be used carefully on muscles which stiffen up suddenly.

Your patience with your child's own efforts and your trust in whatever she attempts alone at her level of development will also build your relationship as well as develop her abilities.

Play ideas are included in all the daily activities as well as during the special times for play. It is through pleasurable activities that your child learns, and so both of you can enjoy carrying out the daily activities as your relationship grows.

5   EATING AND DRINKING

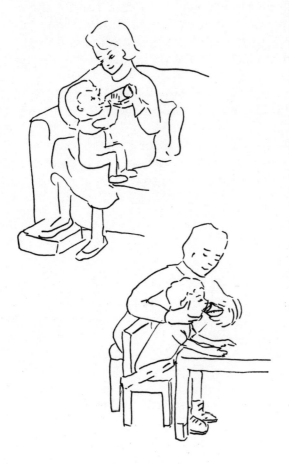

FIRST STAGES

Controlling Posture and Moving

Place your child on your lap, in as upright a position as possible, and later on a chair. Support him around his shoulders with both his arms in front or on a table. A hand on top of his head or supporting him under his chin helps him control his head. He may control his head on his own if he leans forward onto his forearms or grasps a support. Keep his hips well back against you or against the back of a chair. He should sit equally on each of his buttocks with his knees apart and feet flat on a firm surface. Keep his head and body in the middle and bring him forward, bending his hips to control his balance and allow him to participate more easily in drinking and eating.

He may be able to control his posture better in a specially adapted chair recommended by your therapist. The height of the table is adjusted so that it is easier for him to balance, and he can develop the use of his hands later. He may also be able to balance leaning against the ordinary table shared by your family at mealtimes.

Using Hands

Stretch both his elbows if they tend to bend and so that he can catch sight of his hands. His hands are opened or may grasp the opposite edge of the table, a horizontal bar or an upright rod attached where he can stretch and reach them.

Begin to develop his interest in placing or patting his open hands on the bottle or cup. Either hold his wrists or place his open hands on the bottle or cup. Let him feel the warm temperature. Some children can easily hold the bottle later if it is covered in a striped towel, which they can also see more easily. It is also important for your child to feel the warm temperature of the bottle without towelling.

Looking

During feeding your intimate communication and warm relationship develop as you look at each other and are close to each other. You may face your child if you feel more comfortable. The advantage of sitting beside him is that you can bring your face round towards him while you hold him close to your body. There is no hard and fast rule.

Sometimes, before and after feeding, draw his attention to looking at the food, the utensils and his placemat which all show his area for a meal at the table. Use contrasting colours to make each object stand out. For example, have a bright, plain-coloured placemat contrasting with both the table and the utensils. The colour of the food contrasts with his bowl. Bottles or cups stand out if they are covered in black and white tape or towelling, or in bright colours.

For a long time avoid patterned tablecloths, bowls and bibs. It is difficult for him to see your hand actions, the utensils and food against such patterns. Much later he will have to be trained to recognise an object against backgrounds of patterns or of a similar colour.

Listening

Your warm, encouraging voice and enthusiasm for the joys of eating should come before and after the actions of feeding. Your child needs quiet so that he can concentrate on taking the food or trying to use his hands. Find food which also makes interesting noises in the bowl or in his hands, such as cereal flakes or crisps.

Sensing

Keep your child close to you, holding him firmly for balance and later when you guide his actions. Your warm, encouraging presence helps him accept new sensations of posture and actions as well as the new tastes, temperatures and textures of foods. Sharp tastes, sudden touching, sudden movement or even a new cup or spoon may provoke a spasm, a thrust backward, gagging or an involuntary bite reflex.

All new sensations should therefore be very gradually introduced with only one new change at a time. If your child's face is hypersensitive to touch, accustom him to this gradually. Place his own hands on his face and mouth. You can stroke his arms towards his face while singing him soothing songs.

Communicating

Let him know when he is going to be touched, picked up and taken to eat. During the meal, warn him when food is approaching by your tone of voice, with the smell of the food, or by shaking the liquid in his bottle, touching the bottle or cup to his lip, and later by tapping the spoon on his bowl and touching the spoon to his teeth or lip. Wait for him to indicate what he would like, how much he wants and how fast or slowly you should feed him. Pause to let him know that you expect him to play an active part in taking his food into his mouth. He then feels more in control and will be more co-operative.

Understanding

Develop your child's understanding not only of the abilities described above but also of the following:

Sucking and swallowing
Move the bottle or breast in and out of his mouth to stimulate this. Push gently against his chest to stop him stiffening backwards. Once again, pause so that he will accept the nipple. In this way, your baby learns to choose the moment when feeding starts.

Maintaining upright position of head in order to take food
Your child develops head control not only to look at you but also to take his food. Offer food from *below* and in the middle of his mouth, so that he can overcome any stiffening, twisting or falling backwards. Expect him to move his head forwards to take his food, gently bringing him towards it to show what you want him to do. You may just need to wait for his head action, which gives you the clue to when he is willing to participate.

Opening his mouth
Wait for this in response to the smell of food, the touch on his lips with the bottle or cup, or when he sees the food near him. He shows by this reaction that he understands. If necessary, gently press his lower lip from below his chin. Do keep his head upright and forward as his mouth opens to assist his control of his upright posture.

Closing lips and swallowing
Help him to do this by pressing his lower lip closed with one finger. Gently stroke along his throat and beneath his chin with your other fingers. Use your fingers and hand of the arm which is encircling his shoulders and holding him close to you.

Put a little liquid in the cup or thicken the liquid so that it does not pour out suddenly. Keep your child's head under control if he tends to drop it forwards or backwards, arch stiffly or turn it frequently to one side only. Leaning onto his forearms and against the table help to prevent these problems.

Taking liquids and strained foods off a spoon
Accustom your child early on to feeling a spoon in his mouth. Offer him pleasant, sticky foods to lick off and his familiar drink to take off the spoon. Some children can be gently encouraged to try mashed or strained foods near the end of these stages, in much the same way as able-bodied babies are weaned onto such foods. The earlier that semi-solids can be introduced the better. However, do check that there is no

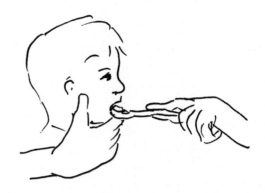

medical reason to stop you introducing semi-solids. If your child tends to bite involuntarily, place a spoon of unbreakable plastic or horn into the side of his mouth between his teeth. If he involuntarily thrusts out his tongue, make sure you press the spoon down firmly and gently push down and back on the middle of his tongue. This helps him to retract his tongue and swallow.

This 'tongue-thrusting' may happen with food he likes! If it only happens with food he does not want, then it is a voluntary action and a protest which you can deal with in much the same way as you would with able children. Tongue-thrusting should not be used to lick food or it will increase. As you help your child develop chewing in the next stages, he will get over these bite responses and tongue-thrusts, and problems with drooling will also diminish.

REMEMBER: To keep as calm and relaxed as you can to reassure your child, since learning to drink and eat often takes a long time. Patience is needed by both of you.

Mealtimes
A child first needs quiet, unhurried feeding sessions alone with his mother or special carer with whom he is making contact and developing a close rapport. In the security of this relationship and in the familiar, predictable way in which he is fed, you can help him to learn all the abilities he can.

Naturally, he should also increasingly be present at family or school mealtimes, watching, listening and being talked to. If he can he might eat a biscuit or hold a spoon while his mother is busy with the family. It is helpful if he learns that family and friends enjoy eating. However, he may not see them well enough to imitate how he should feed himself.

SECOND STAGES

Controlling Posture and Moving

Gradually decrease support of your child, remove any supporting straps or gently remove the support of the table edge from his body. Occasionally he may find it easier to learn to feed himself if he is well-supported in a standing apparatus in front of a table. He will welcome having your body near him, so make sure that any equipment does not isolate him from you.

Using Hands

He may now use one hand to eat while the other remains on the table or grasping the bar for support if he is unsteady when sitting. He can see the hand on the table and can use it to lean on, to grasp a bar and later to grasp and hold his bowl. See 'Understanding' in this and the next stage for more use of hands.

Looking

Continue as in First Stages. You might playfully get your child to follow his shiny spoon 'flying in' slowly to his mouth. Although he can now wait longer for his food, make sure that he enjoys the game! Encourage him in your own way to look at you as you bring his food, as well as to watch it come from his bowl to his mouth.

Listening

Continue as in First Stages. Near the end of this stage and in the next, begin helping your child to look towards the sound you make with the liquid in his cup, or by tapping it on the table near him. Later guide him to reach along the table surface to find the noise of the cup or a spoon. Keep the cup or spoon stationary *at the same spot until he finds it*. Do this naturally, just before you give him the drink or food, a few times during a meal.

Sensing

Your child will be more attentive to his sense of balance and to all his senses when using his hands. Help him look to where he touches and smells. Finger-feeding is therefore of particular value. He is now developing and enjoying more mouth sensations of tastes, textures and movements.

Communicating

All feeding movements contribute to the development of speech by exercising mouth muscles, as well as to interaction with you. Your child may scream if he dislikes certain foods. Show him how to shake his head or push you away, rather than scream, and follow this with what he wants. Perhaps you have another approach to teach him to use a more socially acceptable communication than screaming. Remember, many children are fussy or protest at mealtimes; it is normal and not always due to their disabilities. At these stages you begin to show your child how to respond to 'No' by physically stopping him from, say, throwing the bowl of food away from him. Perhaps he can understand some simple gesture and word, together with the previous Stage's warnings or clues that food is arriving. From now onwards he may see or understand a gesture or sign that means 'eating' or 'drinking'. In your natural tone of voice you say, 'Here's your food,' or, 'Open your mouth,' and can begin to expect his understanding to grow. You may say what you are doing if this does not distract him from what he is concentrating on.

It is important to teach your child to choose between a drink or some food, or between types of food, by looking at or pointing to what he wants. This also increases his collaboration with you, as well as developing his use of his vision and hands.

Understanding

Holding the bottle or cup
With your child's elbows supported on the table, develop the action of holding the bottle or cup with both hands so that a weaker hand is also exercised. Either open both hands on the cup or place his hands onto easy-to-hold handles on a cup. If you press his wrists down his grasp increases.

Taking the bottle or cup to his mouth
From behind your child, guide the bottle or cup to his mouth and wait for him to drink, then guide his hands back to the table. When you are behind or slightly behind him, it allows him to feel the precise natural movements for drinking which he will begin to take over after a period of time. Sometimes pressing down on top of his shoulder steadies his elbow so that he can take over more easily. Gradually release your guidance, first of your child holding the bottle or cup, and then of his movements from table to mouth. See what he manages first. Gradually let go just before the bottle or cup reaches his mouth and then when it is farther and farther away. At first guide your child's hand or wrist and then progress to guiding from his elbow or shoulder.

Picking up bottle and cup
Guide him as he reaches or searches for the bottle or cup, always in the same place on the table. Use the ideas given in 'Listening'. Show him a patting touching action

45

with his hand along the table surface to find his cup. Use whatever vision he has. Encourage more reaching and searching at other times, so that he feels all parts of the table and all edges. Once he can find his cup, playfully help him reach for it at other parts of the table.

As he reaches out, he is stretching bent arms, elbows, wrists and fingers. Help him take the cup and continue his developing ability to bring it to his mouth. You may hold the base of the cup only. Make picking up the cup easier by having a lid on it and standing it on a non-slip mat. Have your child shake his bottle, or cup with lid, to create familiar sounds.

Taking bottle or cup to mouth and drinking

Develop this skill further from the First Stages. Use more liquid so that the cup becomes heavier and demands more control for liquid to flow. A cup with a round cut-out on the side opposite your child's lips helps him see the liquid coming and prevents his little face and nose disappearing inside the cup! At this stage you must continue to replace the cup on the table. Your child will develop this ability later.

Offering biscuit to mouth; introduce thickening and a few solids to meal

Very gradually thicken milk, add mashed foods and a few minced solids. Some children take longer than others to accept new food, but without our forcing too much, not expecting much at every meal, they will eventually accept this. Dip the biscuit in his favourite or familiar drink at first, and keep as many other things as familiar as possible. Mix new food lumps well with your child's familiar liquids to a consistency he will accept. Do continue to persist with the introduction of solids from as early as five to seven months of age, as weaning becomes more difficult the older a child grows. Check that there is no medical reason preventing the introduction of solids.

Taking a biscuit to his mouth and biting

Your child may develop either the taking or the holding or even the biting first, before he masters the whole sequence of holding a biscuit, taking it to his mouth and biting it. Hold the end of the biscuit or rusk, pulling it slightly against his biting action to develop his bite. Later you may use this method for other solids such as meat or fruit.

Chewing

This is assisted by the introduction of solids. Help him chew by massaging his jaw and moving his cheeks, but do not try to determine his chewing rhythm. Keep his lips closed so that his own chewing action and rhythm develop. Let him feel your face when you chew and apparently enjoy your food. Give him very small mouthfuls. Always make sure he has not left any food stuck up against his palate before you lie him down. Should he begin to choke, turn him upside down and pull out the food from his mouth. Ask your therapist to show you what to do on those very rare occasions when this may happen, so that you can relax and help your child chew.

Holding a spoon and taking a spoon
A thicker handle on a spoon may help him
grasp. Press firmly on his wrist and fingertips so that he can maintain his grasp,
removing your help as soon as he develops
his grasp (see illustration). Sometimes your
firm pressure on his shoulder on either side
will help his control of sitting and hand-to-
mouth action, allowing him to concentrate
on holding and later taking the spoon or
other utensil. A strap across his hand and
attached to the spoon handle may be necessary. Some children can manage better with
a long-handled spoon which you also grasp
next to his hand to guide the spoon and
hold on to it if he does not maintain his grip
all the way.

Stroke the outside of his hand or along the
front of his fingers to stimulate him to open
his hand and take the spoon. Leave him to
hold and play with it, and show him how
to bang and scrape it on a safe surface so
that he gets to know it on his own terms.

Taking spoon to mouth with help, but cannot yet replace it
Continuing releasing your help as in First Stages. Scoop food onto the spoon and let
him take the spoon alone to his mouth. You follow, replacing the spoon in his bowl
of food. Begin to use a heavy, high-sided bowl on a non-slip mat, so that this becomes
familiar to your child for use in the next stage.

Finger and hand feeding
Continue hand-to-mouth action with this
important stage. Using hands and fingers
develops during finger feeding. 'Messing'
helps him to get to know the textures and
temperatures of foods which cannot easily
be seen or understood. At first he opens his
whole hand to push food into his mouth
and later he becomes more precise. Progress to putting just one or two of his
fingers in food as you hold his other fingers.
Show him how to lick sticky food off his
index finger. All this 'messing', seeing his
fingers covered in food, helps him to get to
know his hands as well as his food.

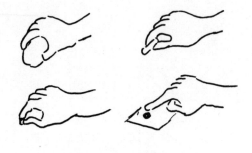

Encourage your child to pick up or hold small pieces of food. You may have to guide him in this, making sure he looks and finds the pieces of food against a contrasting coloured bowl or table.

Wiping mouth
Use a warm, wet facecloth in your child's hand and show him how to take this to his mouth and how to wipe it. Patting your child's mouth with the facecloth also stimulates his mouth muscles, which prevents drooling.

Mouth movements
After eating, stroke, tap and gently stretch his lips as an exercise for his speech muscles. If he can, encourage him playfully to make sounds with you as well. Take turns in making sounds and smiling at each other, so helping both communication and understanding.

Passing from hand to hand
Once your child can hold with both his hands, guide him to pass his cup from hand to hand. Do the same with the facecloth, biscuit or a piece of fruit. Press down on the top of his hand to stimulate it to let go of what is stuck in his hand.

THIRD STAGES

Controlling Posture

Expect him to be sitting alone while using his hands. Try supported standing while eating or drinking. Some children have found it easier to eat while supported in a standing frame.

Using Hands

Offer your child food in the air near the table, then farther and farther above it. Later still, offer him his bowl of food from behind, so that he has to turn round, reach out, maintain his balance, take the bowl and place it on his table. Since this sequence needs a lot of control, you may have to guide or support him. Continue to establish previous abilities from the First and Second Stages.

Looking

Encourage him to look towards a cup or biscuit being offered from either side of him, from above and from below, and later from behind him. Use a friendly voice or other sound to help at first. Keep food stationary when he tries to reach for it, then always give it to him. Encourage him to watch you bringing his food from farther away. Call him and then bring it silently as he watches you.

Listening

Do the same as looking. Without seeing the source of any sound, your child will take time to learn to turn to it and after that reach for it. He needs practice to turn to your voice, the sound of liquid in his cup, or the tapping of his spoon. Have someone turn his body in the direction of the noise. Then your child can learn to turn on his own. After that he will learn to look up or down, or behind, to find the source of a sound. Naturally do this only once or twice at each meal and practise more during play with toys, with your voice, and with the voices of family members.

Sensing

Have your child with you as you prepare meals in the kitchen. Help him notice the sounds of different foods as he tastes, smells, handles and eats them.

Communicating

By now he may understand more natural gestures, signs and words. Discuss special signing with your child's speech therapist. He may be shown some gestures or special signs with words to precede 'eating' or 'drinking' before this is done. He may now be able to say what is 'hot' or 'cold', 'give me', 'no', 'yes', 'thank you' or to ask for more. However, speech development is highly individual and needs further discussion with the speech therapist and psychologist.

Understanding

Develop the following actions at this stage:

Holding spoon and eating
Establish this independent ability with practice, but still guide your child in overcoming a normal tipping over of the spoon and spilling. Guide replacing of spoon less and less.

Scooping food onto spoon after replacing spoon in bowl
Guide him less with spoon replacement but give him more help with scooping. Put food near the high side of the bowl and guide him to scoop against that. You might help him tip the bowl to help the scoop, if his hand use is adequate. If his sight is very poor, teach him to touch and feel food go into his spoon. He may like to have a spoon in one hand and also hand or finger feed with the other. Scooping food takes your child much longer to achieve due to his multiple disabilities.

Mouthing utensils and other objects on the table
This continues for quite some time as your child needs to get to know what he cannot see or handle well. In the next stage it can be decreased as he is able to understand and use his hands more. If you then distract him by offering him another activity, mouthing a utensil or his hands is discouraged. So show him how to move utensils by placing his hand on top of yours while you use any utensil, or guide his exploration of what to do. Perhaps play a game in which he feeds you with the utensils.

Locating food and utensils
Improve this by dropping food with a 'plop' on different parts of a tray or table. Help your child search for the food at first. Let him search for smaller and smaller pieces, so that he uses finer and finer grasps to pick them up. Show him where to find his spoon—always placed next to his bowl on his place-mat. Later show him how to find the edge of his non-slip place-mat along the side of the table, so that he can use this in future to find his place at the family table on his own.

Putting food in and out of containers
Guide him in finding his biscuits, raisins or fruit inside a container. He can take them out and later put them back again. Wait for him to feel for the food in a container. Continue to get him to feel for the food in his bowl or the liquid in his cup. Guide him in releasing food with his fingers. At first remove the lids of containers for him and later teach him how to do this.

Changing from a bottle to a cup
In certain children this takes place in this stage rather more than in the previous one. You may have been using a feeder cup with a spout and lid in the Second Stage to help make this change. Remove the lid of this familiar cup and use it for drinking as he holds its handles. Teach drinking as discussed in the previous Stages. When weaning your child from his bottle there will be occasional day and night use until the bottle is finally given up.

Throwing and banging utensils
Expect a child with disabilities to prolong this experience more than usual as he takes time to learn what things can do, to practise hand actions, to discover how far it is to the floor and perhaps to see how to control adults! Meanwhile encourage him to bang drums, use hammer toys and also to drop objects into noisy containers. This helps to curtail this stage somewhat. Also tie utensils to the table so that you can forget about having to pick things up.

Mealtimes
By now your child is sharing family mealtimes which offer a pleasurable, intimate experience for him. All his senses are alerted by the food and family communication. He can begin to make his own choices and participate at his own particular level. He will begin to understand the names of foods, family members and situations. His relatives should address him by name and talk to him, but without making him the centre of attention. Should mealtimes be too noisy or boisterous, then gradually build up his time with the family.

FOURTH STAGES

At these stages a child develops the following with your guidance when he needs it:

- Using a fork.
- Using a fork and spoon together.
- Using a knife in play with plasticine, dough or spreading butter or jam, progressing to using it to cut his food under guidance.
- Eating with a knife and fork takes children without problems until the age of four years, which is a long time after this stage.

Consult your occupational therapist and other professionals about special feeding aids and further advice. Other parents can be very helpful and reassuring that children can achieve eating and drinking to a large extent, despite the difficulties.

ANNE

Anne sits on her father's lap, leaning her body against the table. Her father places her hands round both handles of a cup as she cannot yet take hold of them herself. She leans on her elbows on the table, which makes her feel more stable and gives her an idea where the cup comes from as she hears it hit the table after each drink. She can take the cup to her mouth, drink and put the cup down again to hit the table.

Her father shows her how to lower the cup more slowly, and holds it for her as she opens her stiff hands to let go of it. As she opens her hands her arms fly up and she falls. Her father tips her farther forward onto her elbows and presses her shoulders down to keep her elbows stable. He repeats the drinking activity and presses on her shoulders and elbows as she controls her hands when releasing the handles of the cup. This is done at each meal and soon she manages to control her sitting and arms better. All this develops in the presence of her calm and caring father.

Anne understands how to drink as in Fourth Stages, but her hand function still needs development as in Second Stages. Sitting needs practice as in First and Second Stages, but progress is likely as she understands what she should do to control herself while having a drink at every meal.

MARTIN

Martin uses his hands to play with food, rubbing, smearing and throwing it. He uses his fingers to play with food and takes them to his mouth to lick off the food. His carer gives him a spoon to grasp but he bangs it on the table and then drops it, going back to playing with his food with his fingers. His carer then guides his hand grasping the spoon into his bowl of food and brings the spoonful of food to his mouth. She waits— and he waits, not understanding what is happening. She then gently taps his lip, waiting for his cues that will tell her when he is willing to take his food. Feeling hungry helps him actively take the food.

This is repeated many times over for some weeks until Martin comes to understand that this is another way of obtaining food. Up until now Martin had remained playing with his food and finger-licking as nobody had shown him what else he might develop. His hand function was physically at Third Stage as he had finger actions and fine grasps, but his understanding was still in Second Stages.

6 WASHING

FIRST STAGES

Controlling Posture and Moving

Lying on her side
Keep your child's head forward with her chin in so that she can see her body. Both her eyes should be uncovered. Place her arms well away from her body with her hands in line with her eyes. If her uppermost leg turns in and crosses towards the other leg in this *and* in other positions, place it up on a large rubber toy, between her knees. To complete washing or drying, slowly roll her over onto her other side. Bring her arm and head, or her bent legs, over to the other side so that she has to roll over the rest of her body.

Much later, if her sitting balance is still unsteady, she can use this rolling from side to side to wash and dry herself. Fully bend and stretch her arms and legs as you wash them.

Lying on her stomach
Your child may need your friendly persuasion to accept this position. She may like lying across your lap or on a wedge, having you stroke her back with soapsuds, oil or powder. Place her arms over the edge of your lap so that she can lean on her elbows, see her hands and stretch them along a surface to search and reach for, say, the soap container or other bathroom objects.

Encourage her to look up and later reach up to a friendly face or attractive object, so stretching out her body and legs at the same time. Should her legs stiffen and press together, hang them over the edge of your lap and have them well apart on either side of a toy. Roll her from side to side as you wash her different body parts. Begin to encourage her to take her weight through her knees as she lies across your lap.

Lying on her back
This is likely to be more advanced as she has to obtain control of startles, stiffening, twisting to one side or involuntary movements which may be provoked in this position. Train her to hold her head and body straight with her head supported on towels or well up on a wedge. This also helps her to see what is happening. Assist lifting of her arm or leg in this position, with her hips held up on a support or in your lap. Bring her arms forward so that her hands touch her body. Bend her knees well up, turning them out to stretch stiff muscles while you wash between her legs.

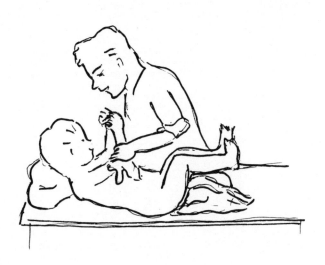

Hold her feet on the surface, raising her hips off a support and later from a flat surface so you can wash underneath.

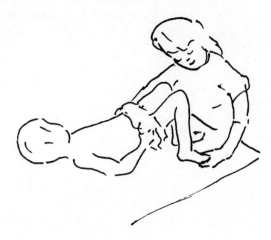

Bring her up from lying on her back to sitting by holding her shoulders forward, looking straight at her face and calling to her to lift her head to get up.

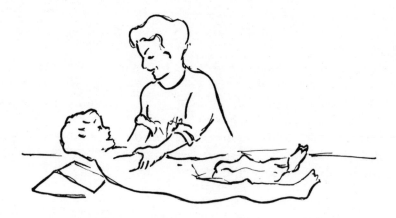

Supported sitting

When lowering her into a bath or bath-seat, hold her bent forward in a sitting position. Have a small distance between your lap and the bath when doing so. Let her immerse a foot or hand in the water before you put her fully into it. All these suggestions reduce startles, fears, or stiffening.

In the bath, fully support your child against a family member's body, or with the bath-seat. Hold her sitting with her body well forward over one of your arms as you wash her back with the other. Leaning forward makes it possible for her to touch her legs or splash and later to lean on her open hands or to grasp a rail. Later on she may sit on a plastic chair in or out of the bath, holding a rail as she is washed. Encourage her to hold her head upright while looking at your face. Sit her equally on each buttock with hips well back, knees apart and, if she is on a seat, keep her feet on a surface.

At a wash basin sit her on your lap or in her wheelchair, leaning against the basin. She can hold on and later put her hands in the water to help. Make sure that she always sits equally on each hip, knees apart, and, if she is on a chair, keep her feet flat on a support.

Supported standing
Fully support her body against yours or on a table. She grasps supports as you wash and dry her. You may use knee splints and well-supporting shoes with her legs apart and with her leaning against a sturdy wash basin. Without these she herself straightens her knees, keeping her feet flat on the floor on a non-slip mat. She is not ready for standing if she overstretches or bends her knees inwards.

Using Hands

If her hands are hypersensitive, soap or rub along her body and arms first, slowly approaching her hands. Move her arms so that she is first to touch her body where she can see best (her area of vision). Stroke the outside edge of her hand with the sponge or towel so that she opens her hand and then grasps it. Avoid forcing anything into her hands. Find ways of making it enjoyable for her to be aware of her hands by patting them together or on her body, as well as by kissing and blowing on them. Let water run over them, and splash them without alarming her—or drenching you! Soap, cream and powder her hands, slowly guiding her wrists so that she can rub her hands together and then rub her own body. Stiff hands open and grasp better if her elbows are straight and her head is straight. Give her a large bunch of towelling or a large rail to grasp with her fingers and thumbs on either side. Press down on her wrists to increase her grasp.

58

Looking

Attract your child's attention to your face before and after washing procedures. During washing she needs to watch your actions, her hands and other body parts as you handle them. Make sure you are in her area of vision, coming close if necessary. Steady her head, holding it on top when she has to look—and when you have a free hand to do so! Use brightly coloured soaps, towels or washcloths which contrast with the colour of you and your hands. Move slowly from side to side, above and below her, so that she follows you with her eyes.

Listening

Amuse her with songs, different tones of voice and gentle, interesting sounds such as that of water and your washing actions. Encourage her to look at your face or hands moving and making a noise in front, to each side, above and below her. You may have to turn her head to do so. Continue this well into the Second Stages.

Sensing

She may enjoy being tickled, blowing, loud kisses and pats along her body and limbs. Use pleasant-smelling soaps, bubble baths, oil and powders. From now onwards accustom her to soft and rough towels, wet and dry washcloths, warm and cold splashes of water. Let her enjoy moving in bath-water, emphasising those movements which she rarely uses.

Communicating

Let her know when she is about to be washed or her position changed. Warn her with the same touch, same phrase or by tapping, say, her soap container on a surface. Have her nearby when you make preparations for washing, such as running the water from a tap or a shower. Bring her to see what makes any sound that might alarm her, and so reassure her. She is learning to anticipate when it is washing time. When you stroke, tickle or kiss her body, stop from time to time to see if she indicates that you should continue. Teach her that if she indicates then something pleasant can happen. Perhaps you can find something else that she likes doing in order to play this game.

Understanding

Besides the growth of understanding of all the other abilities, your child is getting to know you and to enjoy your caring for her. So do make it pleasant for both of you! She also gets to know her body through all the postures, movements and sensations. This prepares her for learning how to wash and dry herself in the future.

More Recommendations for First Stages

1 Offer interesting objects or face her, so that she does not have to look up. Looking up could cause a startle, stiffen her or throw her backwards. You might also support her head and shoulders or expect her to hold on, to lean forward and control her head.

2 She may stiffen if you support the back of her head, press on the soles of her feet or palms of her hands. Give support at her upper neck, round her shoulders or firmly on top of her head. Her own weight on her flat feet or hands when sitting or standing decreases this sensitivity.

3 Give firm support to any posture and stay close to her so that she is given confidence to accept any new sensations and experiences.

4 Begin to follow a routine in washing and drying, so that she learns what will happen next. For example, wash her legs before her body and then wash her arms.

SECOND STAGES

Controlling Posture and Moving

Lying on her side
Your child now leans on her elbows or hands, supported by your lap or a roll of towel. Help her to turn over to the other side to complete washing or drying.

Encourage her to reach out for her foot and to wash and dry it when she is ready to do so.

Bring her up from lying on her side to leaning on her elbow or her hand by pulling gently on her uppermost arm. Guide her to look at you and listen to you and to make active efforts herself to get up. When she understands, expect her to hold out her uppermost arm for washing or drying.

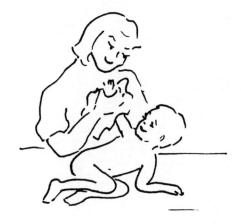

Once she is up, she sits leaning on one or both of her arms while you wash and dry her. Much later she will control her posture as well as use her hand to wash and dry herself.

Lying on her stomach
She leans on one elbow or hand, stretching her other arm or leg out straight in order to be washed or to reach for a toy. Expect her to do this alone once she understands.

Encourage her to get up onto her hands and knees and reach her arm or leg out to be washed and dried. Get her interested in turning to your touch or your voice.

Kneeling

She kneels upright, held against your body as you press her hips as straight as possible. She holds onto your neck, using both arms. Avoid upright kneeling if she cannot straighten her hips yet and overarches her back. Later she may kneel upright, leaning on a chair or holding the chair back or a rail.

Try her kneeling on one knee with her other foot in front and with her bottom first supported by your lap or a low stool. These kneeling postures can be useful for her future washing independence as well as leading to her getting up to standing, improving her balance and decreasing stiff, straight legs.

Lying on her back

Bring her up to sitting, holding her elbows or hands. Show her how to place an elbow or hand down on one side and pull herself up to sitting with the other.

Rolling herself over can now be encouraged during the washing procedure.

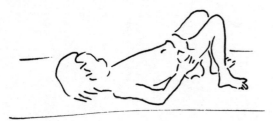

Get her to raise her hips up, keeping her feet flat on a surface so that you can wash her underneath.

Lift her legs towards her face so that she can catch sight of them and stretch out her elbows, and her knees.

Sitting with less and less support
When she is on a chair, give less support so that she learns to control her balance. Bend one knee up and outwards to stretch any tight muscles and to let her see her foot and what is being done.

She may try to hold on with one hand, using the other to play or participate in washing according to her understanding. Press her knees apart and feet well down as she balances, then ask her to do this herself.

She may sit and lean back against the wall, pressing her feet flat on the ground and raising her hips for drying.

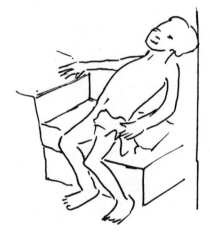

When she sits upright, sway her from hip to hip as each limb is washed or dried. Also sway her forward so that she can pull herself up to standing with your help.

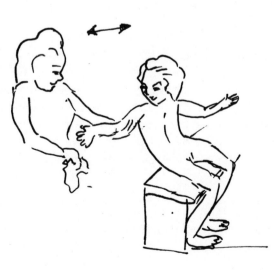

Supported standing
Encourage her to stand equally on each foot, with her body in the middle. She will stand supported while leaning less and less against you or the wash basin, and holding on with only one hand while the other may play or participate in washing according to her understanding.

Sway her from foot to foot in preparation for her putting out a foot for washing. Rest her foot on your lap. She holds on to your shoulders or a rail for support, while you wash and dry her leg. This needs practice as she progresses into the next stages.

Using Hands

Encourage her to reach, touch and grasp her foot, toe, opposite arm or leg so that she will later be able to wash these parts. Find bath toys of many sizes and shapes for her. Place thinner edges of towels between her thumb and fingers to grasp. Perhaps she can grasp and pull the towel away from you. Guide her from behind to pass her washcloth or toy from one hand to another, to hold it with both hands and to drop it—into the bath if possible! She might learn to bang two soap dishes or other objects together, so strengthening her hands further for the time when she can wash herself.

Looking

Keep her looking at you as you move about so that you increase any ability she may have to turn to look at you when you are behind her. Encourage her to watch bath toys float away and towards her, across her line of vision, and show her how to blow them along when she understands more. Encourage her to look at shiny taps or mirrors, especially when you have to carry her farther away from them. Help her look towards attractive bathroom items as you offer them to her, while at the same time she maintains her balance. Give them to her to explore after she looks at them.

Listening

Do the same as for 'Looking' abilities, but emphasise the sounds more. Shake her bottle of lotion or liquid soap in front, to each side and below or above her, first touching her so that she finds it and is given it to hold. In the next stage she will find the bottle without your touch. Show her how to shake it and how to make noises with her other toys and bathroom items—the unbreakable ones!

Sensing

Continue with ideas from the First Stages, adding more of your own. Your child will also sense things by taking them to her mouth, so choose items that are safe to give her. Turn her gently so that she sees where you are touching her, and where she touches herself, with soapsuds, powder or even very muddy hands before she is washed.

Communicating

Continue ideas from the First Stages. Watch for her to show her anticipation of what you will do next when washing or drying in a routine series of steps. Watch for her to anticipate your lifting her up by putting out her arms, wriggling or other action. Perhaps she screws up her face just before you wash it, showing that she is anticipating your action. Respond to any of her indications.

You may naturally talk through what you are doing—'I'm washing your legs'—and may use her name—'I'm wiping Katie's hands'—but she will only understand your words much later. Make sounds in response to any of her sounds, so encouraging her to continue the 'conversation'. She will only copy your sounds much later. Now she responds to your friendly voice, its rhythm and your contact. However, when she concentrates on any particular ability, do not distract her by speaking.

Understanding

Put out an arm or leg for washing or drying
Expect your child to do this first to her front, then to a side, and then later above her head. Make sure that she can keep her balance. She may put her hands together for you to wash them. All this links with the anticipation mentioned under 'Communicating'.

Remove towel from face
Partly cover your child's face or, if she dislikes her face being covered, an arm or foot. She may understand that she can shake it off. Show her how to reach, grasp and

remove the towel for playing a game of 'Where Are You?' Remember, she cannot be expected *fully* to understand the game of 'Peek-a-Boo' or 'Where Are You?' until the next stage.

Getting to know her body
Make sure this is happening during the practical activities in this and other stages.

THIRD STAGES

Controlling Posture and Moving

Establish all the previous postures more securely. Practise more changes in posture to make her future independent washing and drying easier. At first you do the drying while she changes position with whatever support she needs. For example, she is dried from head to hips while sitting on a chair. Get her to stand up, grasping a support, while the lower half of her body is dried. Standing up from sitting in a bath needs practice. One child may need to practise getting dried while kneeling upright, holding a support, then changing to sitting on the mat to dry her feet and legs. Another may start by lying on her back with knees bent, raising her hips for drying and then changing to sitting for drying her upper body and arms and legs. A child may have the ability to dry herself but these position changes must be fully supported by you. See what suits your child.

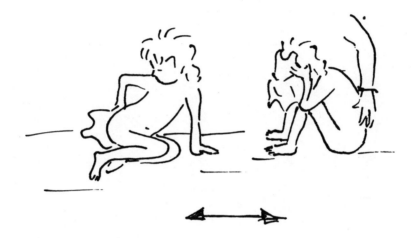

Standing holding on and standing alone
This develops now as you wash and dry your child. She may lift one or both arms above her head. This increases her balance and stretches out her bent arms and her rounded back or body which tends to bend to one side. Standing and turning to reach for a towel or soap also helps such control. She might also try picking up towels from lower and lower chairs.

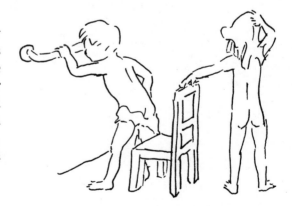

When offering her foot for washing or drying she needs to hold on, but she could try lifting her foot in front and higher into the air. She may lift her foot sideways or up behind her for more standing balance. All this will help her walking, too.

Stepping sideways and stepping forwards
These are both done with your child holding the edge of a bath or basin while reaching for a towel or other article.

Stepping in and out of a bath
Holding on to a rail or the edges of the bath while doing this are ways of building your child's balance control on each foot, improving bending and stretching of her legs and arms as she becomes more independent.

Consult your therapists about using a wheelchair and different types of bathseats. There are many ways in which these can be used, and your therapists will know both your child and your bathroom. Together you will find a solution.

Using Hands

Make time to play whenever you can. Here are some ideas:

- Hold your child's hands resting on a surface. She stretches her finger to prod a piece of soap or make a mark with powder. Perhaps she puts out each finger to be soaped as you hold her first at the edge of a basin.
- Help her finger and thumb to grasp and to place smaller and smaller things, such as pieces of cottonwool or tissue, into and out of containers.
- Hide her hands or feet under bubble bath or soapsuds and help her to find them to be washed.
- Draw her attention to look for anything she drops into the bath or over onto the floor. Have different sizes of plastic bowls for her to drop things into, rather than mess up the floor.

Looking

Continue as in previous stages, also encouraging her to look at smaller and smaller floating objects, cottonwool balls or pieces of tissue. Encourage her to turn and look behind her to reach for her washcloth, for instance.

Listening

Help her to listen for your voice or a splash made behind her where she cannot see. Progress to shaking or tapping a bathroom object above her where she cannot see it. Always keep it stationary so that she can turn and reach or search for it.

Communicating

Your child may now understand a gesture or a few words that let her know she is to be washed. Some words labelling each action may be learnt. Consult your speech therapist and teacher about special signs with which you can communicate if she is deaf and blind or has other problems which prevent her learning the gestures you use. In previous stages your child learnt a warning sound or touch that preceded washing or whatever you were going to do. You may continue using this, especially if she has very poor vision. Later she showed you that she anticipated what was to happen. Now we progress to using gestures, signs and words for communication. Wait for her to use any of these communications to tell you which part of her body she wants to be washed or dried or which toy she chooses to play with.

Understanding (including Sensing)

Your child can now begin to participate in washing, combining all her abilities. Help her learn washing using these ideas:

Break down each washing procedure into smaller steps
Try them yourself to see how you might do it. For example:

WASHING HANDS

1 Maintain sitting, close to a wash basin.
2 Push up sleeves.
3 Put plug in basin.
4 Turn on taps.
5 Feel water level.
6 Turn off taps.
7 Reach for soap.
8 Wet hands with soap.
9 Replace soap.
10 Rub soapy hands.
11 Rinse hands.
12 Pull out plug.
13 Maintain sitting balance throughout.

There may be too many steps or not enough for your child, so adapt the list. You have already encouraged some of these actions in previous stages and are now doing them in a routine sequence *each time*, so that she can join in and learn.

She will find it satisfying *to complete the last step*. She progresses to doing more and more, working back to steps before the last step. She may do whatever she can as she learns all the steps.

Adapt the sequence when your child can only use one hand reliably and the other has to be used as a support. Maintaining balance may be included as a step to be achieved. Changing postures in order to manage various washing or drying sequences may make it possible for her to manage better.

Guide your child from behind or slightly to her side so that she feels your actions in the way she should try and do them. Keep silent as she concentrates on what she is doing.

Share her pleasure in any small achievement, saying how well she is doing.

Once she achieves understanding of the procedure, talk through each of the steps so that words are learnt. Sometimes children respond to your talking through each action as you do it, but at other times they become distracted by your voice. Watch your own child to see what suits her.

Once washing or drying is understood up to a point, try these actions in different postures.

Use equipment if necessary—for example, a magnetic soap holder, soap sewn into a bathmitten, 'soap on a rope' and smaller towels. Keep her washcloth, toothbrush and toothpaste in the same place so that she can remember where to find them.

FOURTH STAGES (*and later*)

All the abilities of posture, movement, looking, listening, sensing, communicating and understanding are developing as you continue training your child's washing actions.

Drying is usually started in these stages.

Train
- Washing face and drying.
- Brushing teeth.
- Brushing nails.
- Grooming hair.
- Washing more of her body.
- Combine washing and drying with dressing.
- Combine washing with finding the bathroom, using her way of getting from place to place.

Use the methods of teaching already discussed.

REMEMBER: It is tempting to do things quickly for your child, but persevere so that she feels she can do it and becomes less dependent on you. There is, after all, much for her to memorise, so it will take time.

Consult your therapist about transfers in and out of baths or showers and about hoists or equipment that may be needed for children who are heavy or who have severe disabilities.

MARY

Mary is a floppy child of 18 months. She has severe visual and learning disabilities with cerebral palsy. She enjoys being washed and prefers lying on her back on a firm surface. Her mother plays at rolling her to each side on soft towels and gradually persuades her to lie on her side supported by waterproof cushions. She accepts being washed in this position and discovers that both her hands can grasp the towels underneath her. She is shown by her mother how to clap and rub her hands with soap.

Some weeks later she accepts being placed on one elbow while she is being washed. She accepts her new posture as her attention is on the washing which she enjoys. Her head flops down but her mother keeps her interest by calling to her and lifting her upper arm to be washed. She looks up to her mother's voice and towards the arm that is being washed. Later still she develops to being able to lean on her arm and she also tries to get up into that posture with her mother's help. As she can now lie on her side and lean on her elbow she loses her fear of doing so and also accepts this position when she is on a rubber mat in a bath with just a little water. Here she discovers that she can kick a leg and splash with the other arm, enjoying the sounds she makes in this way.

Mary is in the First Stages of controlling her posture and moving. She will have to learn to control other postures such as supported sitting, and being on hands and knees over her mother's lap during drying. Later, in the bath she gains control without her mother's full support. Her hearing ability is more advanced and this is used to help her less developed body control. Her mother could encourage her to look at her face when she is in front of Mary, washing her. Many other opportunities for looking can be found in different postures.

CHRIS

Chris is stiff, with both his arms bent and his legs straight. When lying on his back he is too stiff to do anything much to help his carer, though he would like to. When on his side or in a supported sitting position on a plastic chair or supported by leaning forwards over his carer's arm, he *can* help. His legs are now bent and he can stretch out his arms to reach them. His carer can expect him to soap or dry his legs, although she has to guide him at first so that he learns how to do this. Meanwhile she can be washing his back and neck while he is busy with his legs. Later, when being dried on a table, Chris lies on his side and is able to roll over. Once on his stomach his legs are brought over the edge of the table so that he can push himself down onto his feet with his body still lying on the table. While he is standing his feet on a rubber mat, his carer can finish the drying. She can then bring his wheelchair close to him so that he can sit down with her help.

Chris is controlling his posture and moving in the First Stages but he understands how to use his hands in Second and even later stages. He uses his hearing and vision at early stages, depending on his carer being nearby. However, after concentrating on soaping and drying, there are moments when she encourages him to look at her moving about farther away. When drying his feet in a standing posture she talks to him and he turns his head to look down to where she is. The table supports his body so that he can concentrate on this more advanced stage of hearing sound below him.

7 DRESSING

FIRST STAGES

Controlling Posture and Moving

Child lying on her side

Keep her head forward with her chin in so that she sees her body. Both her eyes are uncovered. At first have the eye, ear or hand with better function uppermost. Place her arms well away from her body with her hands in line with her eyes. If her uppermost leg turns in and crosses towards the other leg in this *and* in other positions, place it up on towels or on a large toy between her knees. To complete dressing, slowly roll her over onto her other side. Bring both her arms and head, or her bent legs, over to the other side so that she has to roll over the rest of her body.

Much later, if her balance is still poor, she can use this rolling from side to side to undress or dress herself. Fully bend and stretch her arms and legs as you dress her.

Child lying on her stomach

Your child may need your friendly persuasion to accept this position. She may like lying across your lap or on a wedge rather than on a flat surface. Place her arms over the edge of your lap so that she can lean on her elbows, see her hands and stretch them along a surface to search and reach for her clothes. You may need to guide her arm by the forearm so that she can search along the surface for her clothes. This prepares her for putting out a limb for dressing later.

Encourage her to look up and later reach up to a friendly face or attractive object, so stretching out her body and legs at the same time. Should her legs stiffen and press together, then hang them over the edge of your lap or have them well apart on either side of a toy. Roll her from side to side as you put an arm or leg in or out of her clothes. Begin showing her how to take her weight onto her knees as she lies across your lap.

Child lying on her back
This is likely to be an advanced stage if your child has to obtain control of startles, stiffening, twisting to one side or involuntary movements which are provoked in this position. Train her to hold her head and body in the middle, and straight, with her head supported on a pillow or well up on a wedge. This also helps her see what is happening. Help her to lift her leg or arm into her area of vision by having her hips up on a support or in your lap. Bring her arms forward so that she touches her body.

Also bend each of her legs up and turn it out in order to deal with nappies, socks, shoes and sometimes pants or trousers. This stretches stiff muscles. Later your child uses this position of one leg bent with the foot resting on the other knee as she takes off socks and shoes or puts on pants or trousers in a lying or sitting position.

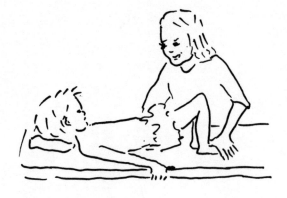

Holding her feet flat on a surface, raise her hips off the support and later off the surface so that her pants can be pulled on or taken off.

Bring her up from a lying position by holding her shoulders or upper arms, tilting her slightly to either side by calling to her to lift her head up.

Child in supported sitting
Fully support her against your body, in the corner of a room or couch, and in a special chair for dressing.

Lean her forward on a small table or over your arm as you undress and dress her. Progress as soon as possible to having her leaning on her elbows on the table or supporting herself with hands and to grasping a rail or the back of a chair.

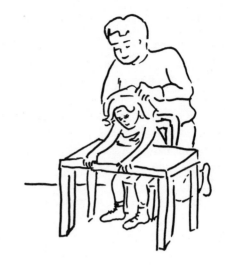

Encourage her to hold her head upright when looking at your face, especially after her head emerges through the neck of her clothing. Put clothing over her face with her head down as this avoids stiffening backwards or startles. When she sits leaning on her arms, have her clothes in front of her, to see and reach when she can control her posture better.

Make sure she sits equally on each buttock, head in the middle, legs apart and, if on a chair, feet flat on the ground. At this stage you may need to tie her hips well back in the chair for support.

Child in supported standing
Fully support her body against you or on a table, with her grasping for support. You may need knee-splints and well-supported shoes to assist her standing without overstretched knees or without having bent or turned-in legs. She herself may straighten her knees, keeping her feet flat and apart. Do keep her standing equally on each foot.

Using Hands

If her hands are sensitive, slide the clothes along her body and arms, slowly approaching her hands. Move her arms so that she is first to pat her clothes in her area of vision. Stroke the outside edge of her hand with some clothing so that she opens her hand and then grasps it. Avoid forcing anything into her hands. Gently make her aware of her hands by patting them on her body, on your hands, and kissing and blowing on them, as well as helping her to feel you. For example, guide her arm so that she moves her hands along your arm to find your fingers. Stiff hands will open and grasp better if her elbows are straight and her head is in the middle. Give her a large bunch of clothing or a large rail to grasp with her fingers and thumbs on either side. Press down on her wrists to increase her grasp.

Looking

Attract your child's attention to your face before and after dressing. During dressing she needs to watch your actions, her hands and her other body parts as you handle them. Make sure you are in her area of vision, coming close if necessary. Steady her head, holding it on top, when you want her to look—and when you have a free hand to do so! Use brightly coloured clothes that contrast with the colour of her hands. Move slowly from side to side, above and below, so that she follows you with her eyes.

Listening

Amuse her with songs, different tones of voice and interesting sounds, such as shoes tapping together, zips or velcro fastenings being opened or clothing materials brushing past her ears. Encourage her to look at your face or hands while you make a noise in front, to each side, above and below her. You may gently have to turn her face for her to do so. Continue this well into the next stage.

Sensing

She may enjoy tickling, blowing, loud kisses and patting along her body and limbs. Use pleasant-smelling talc on her feet to help her socks slide on and off more easily. Emphasise the sliding of clothes along her skin using various textures. However, make sure that she wears comfortable textures close to her skin.

Communicating

Let your child know when she is about to be dressed, her position changed or another item of clothing introduced. Warn her by always using the same gentle touch or voice, or by tapping, say, her shoe on a surface. Have her nearby when you make preparations for dressing, such as opening and closing drawers. Bring her to see what made a sound that might alarm her, and reassure her. She is learning to anticipate when it is dressing time.

When you stroke, tickle or kiss her body, stop from time to time to see if she indicates that you should continue. Teach her that if she does indicate, something pleasant will happen. Perhaps you can think of other ways of playing this game.

Understanding

Besides her growing understanding of all the abilities associated with dressing, she is getting to know you and enjoy your caring for her, so treat these times as special and pleasurable for both of you. She is also getting to know her body through all the postures, movements and sensations. This prepares her for learning how to undress and dress herself in the future.

More Recommendations for First Stages

1   At this stage offer interesting objects or face her so that she does not have to look up. This could cause a startle, stiffen her or throw her backwards. Support her head and shoulders or expect her to hold on and lean forward to control her head.

2   A child may stiffen if you support the back of her head, or press on the soles of her feet or palms of her hands. Support her at her upper neck, round her shoulders, or firmly on top of her head. Her own weight on her flat feet or hands in sitting or standing decreases the sensitivity.

3   Give her firm support in any posture and stay close to her so that she is given confidence to accept any new sensations and experiences.

4   Begin to follow a routine in undressing and dressing so that your child knows what will happen next and later help when she becomes able to do so. For example, her top clothes first and pants next.

5   Put the more impaired arm or leg in first when dressing. Pull them out last when undressing.

6   Pull sleeves along her arm rather than pulling her hands and fingers through. This avoids her stiffening up.

SECOND STAGES

Controlling Posture and Moving

Lying on her side
Your child now leans on her elbow or hand, supported by a pillow if necessary. Help her turn to the other side to complete undressing or dressing.

She gets up to this posture from lying as you pull her uppermost arm towards you. She is also encouraged to reach for what she wants and to put out this uppermost arm for dressing when she understands this.

Once up, she later sits leaning on one or both of her arms while you dress her. Fully bend and stretch arms and legs during dressing.

Lying on her stomach
She leans on an elbow or hand, stretching out the other to reach and for dressing when she understands this. Try this on her hands and knees across your lap and progress to other kneeling postures. Have her turn to your voice and roll or reach towards you during dressing.

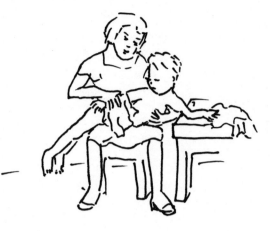

Encourage her to stretch out a leg for dressing as she balances on hands and knees.

Kneeling
She kneels upright held against your body as you press her hips straight. She holds onto your neck. Avoid kneeling if she cannot straighten her hips and overarches her back.

Later she kneels upright leaning on a chair seat or holding the chair back or rail. Try her kneeling on one knee with the other foot in front, with her bottom first supported by your lap or a low stool. She looks down at her feet as socks and shoes are managed. These kneeling postures can be useful for her future dressing independence, as well as leading to her getting up to standing, improving balance and decreasing stiff, straight legs.

Lying on her back
Bring her up to sitting holding her elbows or hands. Show her how to place one elbow or hand down on one side and pull herself up to sitting with the other hand.

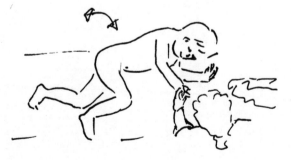

You can now encourage her to roll herself over during dressing. Encourage her to roll towards a sound or your touch when possible.

She raises her hips, keeping her feet flat on a surface, to help you and later to dress herself. Lying flat, she can continue to lift a leg to pull off socks.

Sitting with less and less support
She holds on with one hand, using the other to play or help with dressing according to her understanding. When she is on a chair, press her knees and feet well down so that she balances, and ask her to do so herself.

She may sit and lean back against a high-backed couch or wall, pressing her feet flat on the ground and raising her hips for pulling pants on or off.

She may now lean less and less on the table and even sit and dress without it. Place her clothes in front of her on another chair. Later she can use this chair to hold on to if she can stand up to manage pants or a skirt. She obtains control if she first leans forward, bringing her arms down during dressing and undressing. Later her arms are brought upwards.

85

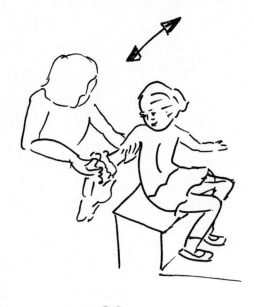

Continue to stimulate her, swaying slightly from hip to hip as each arm or leg on the opposite side is dressed. This also develops some body control for walking. Also sway her well forward when preparing her to stand from a sitting position.

Standing with less and less support
She leans against you or the bed and holds on with only one hand while she uses the other for undressing according to her understanding.

Sway her slightly from foot to foot to prepare her for putting out a foot for a sock, shoe or trouser leg. Give her support and rest her foot on your lap. She holds onto your shoulders or a chair for support. This needs practice into the next stage. When she pulls clothes off her head, support her body and then later her hips as she does so. To do this she gains her own control by first bringing her arms forward and down and later upwards.

Using Hands

Encourage her to reach, touch and grasp items of clothing as well as her feet, toes, opposite arm and leg, as she will later use these actions for dressing. Guide her to slide large rings of clothing material, bangles or cardboard along her arms or legs. Guide her to push her sleeves up or down, but you complete the dressing until she understands. Encourage her to pass a sock or other article from hand to hand, to hold it with both hands and to drop it and find it with help. She might learn to bang her shoes together, so further developing her hands for future dressing. Place thinner edges of clothing, like the top of her skirt or pants, between her thumb and fingers. Guide her to grasp and push or grasp and pull as you continue and complete the dressing action until she understands it.

Looking

Continue encouraging her to look at you moving about, and increase her ability to turn to look at you above, below or at her sides. Talk to her so that she watches you bringing her clothes or putting them away. She maintains her balance as she looks and takes items of clothing offered to her above, below, at the side and behind her. Give them to her to explore after she looks at them. Touch her with the clothes at first if she cannot see or hear well until she can find them in later stages.

Listening

Do the same as for looking abilities, but emphasise the sounds more. Bang her shoes together or call her to find you in front, at each side, below or above her. At first touch her so that she finds you or the shoes and is given them to hold. In the next stage she learns to find what made the noise if she cannot immediately see it. You may begin guiding her to find your voice or tapping a shoe if the sound is near her fingers. Remember to keep the sound in one spot so that she learns exactly where it comes from.

Sensing

Continue the ideas from First Stages, adding more of your own. Your child will also sense things by taking them to her mouth, so choose what you give her with safety in mind. Turn her gently to see where you touch her and where she touches herself when dressing. You may need to guide her hand to where you touch her or kiss her in a playful game. This helps her develop the important localisation of touch which is more difficult when vision is poor.

Communicating

Continue First Stages. Watch for her to show her anticipation of what you will do next when dressing, following a routine series of steps. Watch for her to anticipate your lifting her up by, for example, putting out her arms, wriggling or some other action.

Perhaps she turns away just before you put some garment onto her head. Respond to any of her indications. You may naturally talk through what you are doing—'Mummy is taking off your socks' or 'I'm putting on Christine's dress'—but she will only understand your words much later. Now she responds to your friendly voice and its rhythm and your contact. When she concentrates on any particular ability, do not distract her by speaking. Make sounds in response to any of her sounds, so encouraging her to continue such a 'conversation'. She may only cope much later with taking turns to make sounds.

It is helpful to her understanding of speech if she hears the same phrase repeated to accompany an action of dressing, such as 'arm out' or 'off it comes'.

Understanding

Put out an arm or leg for dressing
At first you may need to guide her arm along a table surface before she can hold it out in the air. Expect her to do this first at the front, then to the side and later above her head. Make sure she can maintain her balance. She may do this more with her unimpaired limb, so wait for it with the other. This is especially important as you will put her more impaired limb in first when dressing her. Expect her to put her head down to anticipate putting on her tops or taking them off. Having her head down prevents her stiffening or falling back when her eyes are covered. All this links with Communicating mentioned above.

Remove clothing from face
Partly cover her face or arm or foot and help her understand how to shake the clothing off or pull it off. Play 'Where Are You?' or 'Peek-a-Boo', but only expect full understanding of this in the next stages. She is now getting to know her body and understanding how it relates to dressing, and this awareness will grow well into the later stages.

Relating two things together is an understanding which is developed during her participation in dressing. She relates sock and foot, sock and shoe or hat and head.

THIRD STAGES

Controlling Posture and Moving

Practise further changes of posture which will make her future independent dressing easier. At first you do the dressing while she changes position with any help she needs. For example, she may find it possible to pull down her pants (or trousers) while sitting, then stand up, grasping a support. Another child may pull down her pants while kneeling upright, then sit down on the floor or on a low chair to complete the removal of the pants. Yet another child may remove her pants while lying on her back with her knees bent, feet flat and hips raised up. From this posture she will get up to a sitting position to complete the removal of the pants. These changes of posture are also useful for putting on her top clothes or dresses. A child may have the ability to understand undressing and dressing but not be stable enough for this while standing. But until her understanding develops it is good exercise for her to control her changes of posture at this stage, while you do most of the dressing. See which ways may suit your own child and together work out your own methods.

Standing holding on and standing alone
This may develop now as you dress your child. With and without holding on, she lifts both or one of her arms above her head for dressing. This increases her balance and stretches out bent arms and rounded backs. Standing and turning to reach for a garment also helps such control. She can also try picking up clothes from lower and lower drawers or stools.

When offering a foot for a sock or shoe, she still holds on but lifts her foot higher, well off your lap. She may lift her foot to the side and up to the back for more standing balance, which will help walking.

Stepping sideways and stepping forwards
These are both used in her efforts to fetch clothes or to go to where she is dressing. Give support if needed.

Using Hands

She is now pointing her index finger through, say, a buttonhole. Hold her fist against a surface so that she stretches out each finger.

Use her finger and thumb to hold thin edges or buttons. At this stage she may pull off loose clothing that is fully unfastened. She may grasp and pull off socks or unfastened shoes. She may put a hat on or take it off. Guide her to do these things if necessary.

Hide her hand or another part of her body under clothing and encourage her to find it. Help her look where she drops clothes or her shoe. If possible she may be encouraged to go and find them and even tidy up!

Continue to show her how to search for a shoe when she drops it. She slides her hand or fingers along the floor until she makes contact and finds it. Keep all this playful, giving her time to concentrate on the game.

Looking

Continue as in the last stages, encouraging her also to look at smaller fastenings. Encourage her to turn and look more behind her and also to reach for whatever piece of clothing you hold up in front, at the side or behind her.

Listening

Encourage her to listen to your voice, or gently tap one of her shoes behind her where she cannot see you approach. Approach above her head, behind, each side and well behind her. Keep it tapping on and off in one place so that she can turn to reach for it. Avoid moving 'the sound' of her shoe into her hand as this will make it confusing for her to learn exactly where it is.

Communicating

Your child may understand natural gestures and a few words telling her what you are going to do. At first she learns more easily if you and family members use the same phrase for actions of dressing. Also, to help her understand, use names rather than he/she, yours/mine and use Mummy/Daddy. She may learn which words describe what you are doing and the names of body parts. Other means of signing for a deaf and blind child or for a child with other problems should be discussed with your teacher and speech therapist. In previous stages your child learned that a touch or sound forewarned her that you were going to do something with her. She then showed you a response or gesture in anticipation of what you were about to do. Now progress is made to words with gestures which precede what will be done for dressing. It is easier for your child to understand phrases about real activities, such as dressing, as she actually does them.

Understanding

Your child can begin to participate in *undressing* herself and progress to dressing—see 'Using Hands'. Help her learn using these ideas.

Break down each dressing procedure into small steps. Try doing them yourself to see how you might do it. For example:

PULLING OFF PANTS
1 Maintain posture in standing position, grasping support.
2 Grasp top of pants with one hand.

3   Push pants down over hips.
4   Repeat this with other hand.
5   Push pants all the way down.
6   Step out of pants.

Another example for taking off an *unfastened* blouse or shirt which unfastens all the way down in front:

1   Child sits or stands securely.
2   Remove sleeve from one arm part of the way.
3   Remove the sleeve from this arm all the way.
4   Remove the other sleeve part way.
5   Remove the other sleeve all the way.

These steps may be too many or too few for your child.

More Recommendations for Third Stages

Your child often finds it satisfying to complete the last part of the whole procedure. She can progress to doing more and more steps until she does the whole procedure from the beginning. She may take one step at a time, doing a step before the last part of the sequence and so on back to the beginning. Perhaps she does what she can in early steps of the dressing procedure, joining in where she can up to the final part.

Use any sequence of steps as a rough guide and make your own adaptations. One child may only be able to use mainly one hand. Another cannot put her arms behind her back and needs a table in front to help. Yet another can manage by changing her postures as practised in the Third Stages. Work out different ways of working, encouraging your child to find her own. Your occupational therapist will suggest more ideas.

Guide your child from behind or slightly to her side, keeping relatively silent as she concentrates on what she is doing.

Share her pleasure in any small achievement, saying how well she has done. Do point out small achievements if she is unaware of them.

Once she achieves understanding of the procedure, talk through each of the steps so that she learns the relevant words. Some children may respond on one occasion to your talking through each action you do but on another may become distracted by your voice. Use the same phrase as other family members to help her learn the words.

Use simple clothing with large arm and neck openings. Front fastenings with larger buttons should be used when your child attempts dressing. Special adaptations may be suggested by your occupational therapist. You may patch clothing where there is more rubbing due to crawling, bottom shuffling or due to crutches. These patches on knees, hips, under arms or on elbows also serve as orientation labels when she learns to dress, to indicate where clothing should be placed on her body. Textured tags may also be sewn onto garments to label top, bottom, back or front. Clothing can be selected by texture if she cannot see or understand colours. It helps if shoes can be laced down to the toes for feet that are difficult to straighten into a shoe.

FOURTH STAGES (*and later*)

Continue training of Stage Three, progressing to the following:

- Taking off jumpers.
- Taking off pants, trousers.
- Putting on various items of clothing (finding armholes, neck, top and bottom).
- Putting on socks and shoes.
- Undoing fasteners (zips, press-studs, buttons).
- Undoing and doing up laces on shoes.

A child without any disabilities normally takes six years to achieve independent dressing. Therefore much time and patience is required of everyone, but this will be worthwhile for your child.

STEVE

Steve cannot sit and does not understand how to use his hands to dress or undress. He has been dressed in lying positions for some time, but now his carer is trying to dress him in a sitting posture. She brings him up to sitting in a number of different ways to see how he can help. Once sitting and leaning forward with his body supported against a sturdy table, he can maintain sitting momentarily. His carer guides his arms to pull off a vest over his head. He cannot grasp the vest so she holds both his hands on the vest and guides him to pull it. After a few tries he manages the last part of this action on his own. As he pulls the vest well over his head, then forward and down onto the table, he controls his sitting at the same time. Soon he no longer needs to lean his body against the table, although he still keeps his arms on the table during dressing and undressing. As he learns dressing he achieves sitting balance at the same time.

KATHERINE

Katherine can pull off her clothes if they are unfastened and she is sitting on a chair in a corner of her room supported by the walls. She cannot stand alone or walk yet. Her carer now shows her how to sit in the corner but grasp a sturdy chair in front of her, pull herself up to standing and then take off her clothes. She needs to hold on with both hands as she steps out of her pants, but finds that she has to learn to hold on with only one hand for the other dressing procedures. It is explained to her that this difficult way of dressing will practise her standing and give her more chance of walking. It is a challenge and she wants to walk, so both she and her carer plan to try this way from now on. Of course she will also stand when playing, washing and having a drink to obtain still more practice in standing, with and later without support.

8 TOILETING

When it comes to helping a child become dry and clean, not only is every child completely individual, but each family is different. Professionals may also have differing views on how best to teach a child control. The following guidelines are for you to weigh up, using your own knowledge of your child. Make a plan with your teacher or therapist, which suits both you and your child.

Consider the readiness of a child for learning toileting on the basis of the following:
1 Ability to sense a full bowel or bladder.
2 Ability physically to control bladder or bowel muscles.
3 Ability to understand what is expected of him or her.
4 Willingness to co-operate.

In addition, children with physical disabilities have to have:
5 Ability to get to the toilet, to sit on the toilet, to manage to lower their pants and to clean themselves.

It may seem unfair to expect children with multiple disabilities to become independent in using the toilet when you consider all these aspects. However, with expectation and training they ultimately achieve various degrees of independence, and in many instances full independence, although only after a long time. This helps their dignity and family life.

It is important to check with your doctor that there is not a medical condition which prevents your child from sensing or controlling his or her bowel or bladder muscles. There are medical workers who will give specialised advice and ways of teaching which help in specific conditions.

Controlling Posture and Moving

Child lying on back

If a child is stiff, turned towards one side or showing involuntary spasms and movements, then have his head supported in the middle and his hips supported by waterproof pillows or your lap. Bend both his knees well and opened outwards. Stretch them as far as possible without causing him discomfort, doing a little more each time. Wash and clean him in this position and later place his feet down, raising his hips to wash underneath him. If possible, expect him to raise his own knees up and press them outwards as well as place his feet flat on the surface and raise his own hips so that you can clean him. He progresses to finding a way he can manage himself. It may not be on his back but in a sitting position with support.

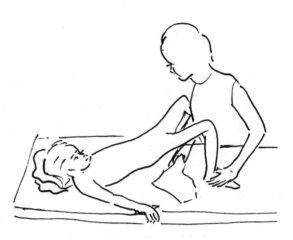

Child in supported sitting position and standing alone

Practise this in all daily activities so that your child has this ability for use in toileting when he is ready.

It is easier for him to sit, holding a rail with both hands in front of him, or to lean on his forearms or hands placed on his own knees, on you, or even flat on the floor. Sitting him on your lap or between your legs makes him feel safe and happy. Squatting or sitting while leaning forward helps him manage his balance and may help him to empty his bowel or bladder. Later, he progresses to sitting more upright. However, at all times he must feel safe, comfortable and stable. Ask your therapist for any special toilet seats or a potty to suit your child.

Sitting, coming up to standing and *sitting down* are also developed in other activities and can be used during toileting. In this way you and later your child can manage his pants before and after toileting. Gently make sure he sits and stands with his body in the middle and his weight taken equally through each side, without bothering him too much.

Using Hands

Hands are used as supports, to grasp and let go of supports, to manage clothes or to play with a toy occasionally. In Chapter 7 various hand grasps are mentioned for managing pants. Training in the understanding of undressing and dressing is also given and can be used during toileting procedures as well.

Looking, Listening, Sensing

Positioning a child with his head up on a support in a lying position, perhaps on his side, and in sitting postures, allows him to see what you are doing to make him feel more comfortable. He comes to understand what he can do to achieve the same.

Communicating

A child may indicate discomfort by crying, by fidgeting, wriggling and later by touching his wet pants or pulling at them or giving some other sign. This shows a growing readiness for starting toilet training, but an increased understanding of cause and effect usually needs development. Your child's other abilities in physically 'holding on', other muscular control and his willingness to participate all need checking before deciding on whether he is in fact 'ready'.

Put him on a stable potty for short times, on your lap or close to you. Accustom him to the feel of the potty or seat of a special toilet, making this as pleasant as possible. Observe his communication about all this and gradually give him time to accept the situation. Let others in the family casually mention and show a child their toileting. Sometimes you may have to avoid flushing the toilet, as this is known to alarm some children with multiple disabilities. Later, when they have overcome their fear, they quite enjoy pulling the chain or pushing the handle.

Understanding

At first a child senses a full bowel or bladder and begins to understand that this leads to the discomfort of soiled or wet pants. Some children take more time than others to recognise this discomfort. However, keeping him clean and dry does help him come to appreciate being this way.

THIRD AND FOURTH STAGES

Controlling Posture and Moving, Using Hands, Looking, Listening, Sensing and Communicating are further developed as suggested in previous stages.

Understanding

Your child may now be ready for independent training. Some suggestions are:
- Keep a record of when your child naturally wets or soils his pants.
- If not, begin an approximate regime in the morning after waking, before and after meals and before going to sleep.
- Put your child on his pot or special toilet seat at these times.
- Sit and talk to your child, holding him so that the experience is pleasant for him.

Do not spend more than five to ten minutes with him on the potty. Should he do something into the pot, give him loving praise. Also give him praise when you later find he is dry.
- Draw his attention to other family members or other children's toileting so that he can see or hear and realise that toileting is everyone's everyday experience.

Later:
- Teach your child a sign to indicate when he wants to go to the toilet. He may be able to say one word or sound.
- Begin teaching him how to locate the bathroom or lavatory.
- Use finding the toilet as an opportunity to practise crawling, bottom-shuffling or walking—when there is time!
- Help your child learn the sequence of finding the toilet, removing his pants, sitting down (or standing if he is a boy), standing up after a short period, putting on pants, going to wash hands and dry them. There are more details in this sequence, especially if wheelchairs are involved. Therefore you will appreciate how much a child needs to remember and that time must be given as he remembers more and more.
- It helps a child remember if you have a routine, showing him the same things in the same way and in the same order each time.
- Consult your therapist about routines of transfer from wheelchair to toilet. There are many ways that will be suggested, so that you and your child can select the most suitable.

Naturally, no scolding or punishment is ever given if toileting is slow or if, despite progress, an occasional wetting or soiling still occurs. Toileting ability may be lost and regained by any child, whether he is able-bodied or not. Discuss with other mothers the many natural reasons for this. Always ignore the times when he does not co-operate or respond by producing something in his potty. However, do recognise when he does co-operate and does do something. It may seem that he will never change, but independence comes, slowly but surely. With practice even children with severe disabilities eventually do what they can and achieve control in late childhood and adolescence. Discuss your worries with other parents and your advisers, since your anxiety is not helpful to your child.

9 PLAY

This chapter adds to your own ideas of playing with your child. Play is a child's work: it is through pleasurable activities that he trains and develops his abilities.

Select different positions for the same play activity. Use stable or well-supported postures when such play activities are more difficult for your child. Find forms of play in which you can use your body close and together with your child, especially when he is little. Progress from these stages to the next.

FIRST STAGES

Controlling Posture and Moving

Child lying on his side
Keep his head forward with his chin in so that he looks at his body. Both his eyes are uncovered. At first have the eye, ear or hand with better function uppermost. Place his arms well away from his body, with his hands in line with his eyes. If his uppermost leg turns in and crosses the other leg in this *and* in other positions, place it up on a large toy between his knees. Have toys sometimes on the floor, sometimes on a low table or sometimes suspended near him. Place toys near his hand or foot or in his area of vision.

Rolling
Roll your child over from side to side in a slow rhythm to relax any stiffness and give him enjoyment of motion. Talk to him and touch him on each side at the level of his ear and shoulder, waiting for him to turn his head to find you. At the same time bring one or both of his arms over towards you to touch you and roll towards you. The rest of his body rolls over as you do this and he overcomes any body stiffening which may happen as he turns his head. You might also teach him to roll over by bringing one or both of his knees over to one side,

allowing him to roll the rest of his body over. Later he learns to roll and find your mouth or a toy which made the sound that attracted him.

Child lying on his stomach
Your child may need friendly persuasion to accept this position. When he is little he will prefer lying across your lap, body or along your body. When facing you or another family member, his hands should be near enough to play with people's faces or hair. As you sing a song, sway him with you from side to side.

An older child can play lying across large cushions or on a padded wedge. Encourage him to raise his head, take his weight through his forearms, then later onto his hands or hands and knees. With your child over your lap, encourage him to bear weight on his knees by pressing your hand down on his bottom. If his legs stiffen and press together, turn them outwards and place them apart by holding his upper legs. When he is on your lap his legs can hang over the edge of your lap. If his upper arms are held stiffly against his body, hold them and stretch them out. Help him play with his hands, stretch them along the surface to search and reach for toys and people nearby.

Sway him forwards and backwards across your lap or on a small beach-ball or roll. Gently increase your sway so that he manages to stretch out his arms and touch the floor and so develops the ability to catch his balance. He may be fearful of this at first, so give him confidence by swaying more gently and allowing him to discover the firm floor first with his hands and then with his feet or knees (on the backward sway). When a child enjoys swaying, and when he has a small amount of head control, give him a swing into the air. Keep smiling and talking to him so that you stimulate him to raise his head and build his confidence.

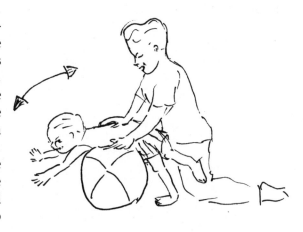

Child lying on his back

Encourage him to keep his head centred and body straight with the help of a pillow up against your knees, or a wedge. He can enjoy watching your face, suspended toys or trees and flowers outside. Interest him in his body by playing with his hands and feet. Assist him to lift stiff or weak legs by having his bottom on your lap or on cushions. When lifting his legs, keep them straight as well as bending them well up and outwards, so that he can touch his feet and later grasp and play with them.

When he is supported by your knees with you lying down, you could play sitting him up and lying back against your bent knees, and then straightening your legs, so that he sinks down full length. You need to support his shoulders so that he can try to lift his head. Later hold his forearms and hands as he succeeds in lifting his head to come face to face with you. You may play bending and stretching his legs as well as opening and closing them. However, avoid any jerky kicking, arching of his body or crossing of his legs. If this does happen he will kick his legs more normally in water or when he lies on his stomach on your lap.

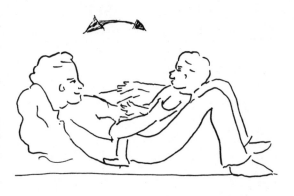

Child in supported sitting
Fully support him against your body, in a corner seat, a corner of the room or of a couch. Lean him forward onto a small table, over your arm or over a supporting cushion. His hands can then touch his legs, his toys and the table or floor surfaces for playful patting, stroking and handling.

He may sit grasping a support with both his hands. Also encourage him to keep his head upright to look at you, toys or a mobile. He will progress to leaning on his elbows on the table, on his hands on a low table or on the floor. However, if he looks down, rounding his back as he listens or when he plays with toys on the floor, you need to lift his arms and place them on cushions or on a table to sit him more upright.

A hand on top of his head helps his control. Ask your therapist about special chairs for him.

Carry him upright in a sitting position on your hip, or with his back to your body to develop upright head control. Also carry him over your shoulder to keep his head up to look at people and objects as you take him past them. Sway him from side to side to amuse him and to stimulate head control.

Child in supported standing

Fully support his body against yours or against a high, sturdy table. He may need knee splints, calipers or a standing frame and well-supported boots to assist standing without overstretched knees or bent and turned-in legs. He may be able to straighten his knees and keep his feet flat on his own. *He is not ready to stand if his legs cannot be corrected yet, or if he is not ready to hold his head and body upright.*

Using Hands

Open hands by pressing the base of your child's wrists against a toy or table and taking his thumb out from his palm. Stiff hands open more easily if his elbows are straight and his head is in the middle. Also stroke the outside edge of his hand or the tips of his fingers with a toy so that he opens his hand to touch and take the toy. Once open, pat his hands together, on his body, on his mouth, and on you. Hold his arms to do this if his hands are very sensitive. Always leave his hands free so that the choice to pat and grasp is his. Gently guide his arm holding his shoulder or forearm until his fingers make contact with you or a toy.

Grasp is developed by gently placing his hands around your finger or a small ball or block that fits into his hand. As he plays with his feet and fingers he develops grasping. As he grasps with one hand, guide his other hand in to touch and grasp as well. Assist him to hold toys with both hands at the same time. Avoid squeezy toys which increase tightness in stiff hands. Help him grasp with fingers and thumb on either side of a toy or handle. Press on his wrists to increase his grasp of objects and rails which he holds for balance.

REMEMBER: Avoid pushing any toys into your child's hand or pressing his fingers around them. This may cause him to withdraw.

106

Looking

Attract your child's attention to your face or those of family members in his field of vision. Play moving your face from side to side, above and below his face, expecting him to follow you as best he can. Move farther away and come up close playing 'Here I am'. Catch his interest by wearing jewellery, bright make-up, a silver paper hat or foil on your nose, or a biscuit in your mouth. At other times use glowing lights, spinning objects, balloons, bubbles or mirrors for him to follow. Shine lights on his body, hand or the floor as you wave them about for him to see. He may follow a tiny torchlight if it does not dazzle him, but a glowing light has more form and interest. Always try to keep him looking at you or the toys when no sound is made. You may have to come very close or keep yourself moving if stationary objects are difficult for him to see. Look at everything together with him so that you communicate enjoyment to each other.

Listening

Amuse your child by changing your tone of voice and varying its loudness. Interest him in sounds around the house, in the garden and countryside. Take him to see the door closing, for example, letters dropping or who it was who made footstep sounds, when he becomes able to understand this, as well as for reassurance about unknown sounds. Amuse him also with the sound of the pat, rub, scrape, scratch or slide actions of the same object. Show him how to make these sounds with the object or toy.

Sensing

Gradually have your child roll over on many different surfaces such as a leather couch, silver and crackly paper, grass, carpet, linoleum, and on a large bed or inflatable mattress. Gently immerse his hands and feet in sand, water, lentils, beans, peas, rice and other interesting objects from the garden or house. Natural objects such as cones, leaves, grass, mud, snow, sachets of strong-smelling herbs or dried flowers are all attractive to children. If necessary, guide him to pick up, touch, handle, smell and taste a variety of objects. Then leave him to explore them in his own ways as well. Let him lick and suck his own hands to discover them, too. Naturally, move anything away which he cannot safely lick or swallow. Gently lift him up in the air and down to a happy sound, to enjoy the feel of movement in space. Support his head if necessary.

Communicating

Everything that you and your child do together enhances your warm communication with each other.

Let him know when he is about to be taken to play, have his position changed or be introduced to a new toy. Warn him with the same gentle touch, voice, phrase or with a gentle tapping of a toy on a surface. Always make your child feel 'invited' and not 'forced' to play.

At the end of this stage and into the next stages, try to take turns in making sounds to-and-fro with your child in a happy 'conversation'. When he makes any sound, repeat this back to him even if his hearing is poor. Breathe your words in a loud whisper into his ear and let him feel the vibration of your throat and chest as you speak and sing. Bounce him and roll him, trying to stimulate any sound during such play with big, easy movements. Also pause during play, to give him the opportunity to indicate that you should continue the game, which you will then do. In these ways he learns that his communication can make something pleasant happen.

Understanding

Every time your child responds to your efforts you appreciate his new growth of understanding of the play activities.

Help his understanding by playing with one toy at a time. Leave a favourite toy in the same place, attached if necessary by string, so that he can find it. He will want to cling to one toy as well as one person at this stage and needs this for longer than children without disabilities. Show him that his favourite toy can also be played with in other satisfying ways besides the one he has discovered.

Some children become overattached to one toy and are distressed when it is removed. Therefore keep coaxing him to take an interest in a variety of other playthings each day. Add new toys which are not too complicated and demand only a short span of concentration.

SECOND STAGES

Controlling Posture and Moving

Child lying on his side
Your child plays leaning on one of his elbows or hands, with support if needed.

To a song you can bring him up to these positions and down again by holding his uppermost arm straight and turned outwards. When you bring him up, wait for him to place his underneath elbow or hand on the surface and push himself up. From lying on his side he may also reach upwards for your face or a toy and so want to get up to sitting, leaning on his other arm.

While lying on his side a child may play pulling bracelets of bells on and off his arm or leg.

Child lying on his stomach
Tip his hip or shoulder, or both, well backwards on each side, enabling him to reach for a noisy or shiny toy. Hold the toy near his hand so that he can actively make contact with it. If you tip him still farther back he may come up to sitting leaning on his underneath arm or hand. If necessary support his body so that he can change his position and feel these possibilities.

Creeping
Tip his hip or shoulder, or both, backwards on each side to stimulate a creeping action of his arm or leg. Have a toy ready for him on the nearby surface so that he makes contact with it. He may then want to creep towards a toy on his own. You can also tip him so that he creeps his arms and legs along your body or across your lap. Perhaps hold his heel steady, though not his sole or forefoot, so that he can push off. Your physiotherapist may have many more ideas to show you for teaching creeping.

Crawling
Play with your child in a crawling position, with his hands and knees supported by your lap or held suspended by a blanket or crawling equipment. As he plays he reaches out in various directions for toys. You might use his reaching forwards towards a toy to start him off crawling forwards. It helps if you sway him from one side to the other as you bring him forwards. Also do this to music, forwards and backwards, and discover whether he may be better crawling backwards.

Build his confidence by having him lie along your body and tip him down to each side. Tilt him well down so that he can catch his balance onto one hand and one knee on the same side. Try this on different surfaces such as beds, floor or grass. Let him feel how far it is to the ground.

Your child may enjoy walking on his hands as you support his hips or his legs. This strengthens both his arms.

Kneeling and knee-walking
From his crawling position your child may want to reach up for a toy on a couch and so come up to kneeling. When playing in a kneeling posture check that his hips are straight, that he does not overarch his back, and that he kneels equally on each leg. Hold both his arms forward or leave them on the couch as you sway him rhythmically from knee to knee so that he can later progress to stepping sideways or forwards. Kneeling upright and stepping backwards with straight hips are desirable for later walking but are more advanced.

From sitting on your lap with one foot flat in front, place his other knee back on the ground. He may support himself on his hands on the floor as he plays without your support. Roll small cars or tins around his ankle. Now or later, he may understand a toy going 'under' his knee or 'over' his foot.

REMEMBER that all crawling and kneeling games must be interspersed with games using postures and movements which stretch out his knees and hips so that he does not stiffen into a bent position.

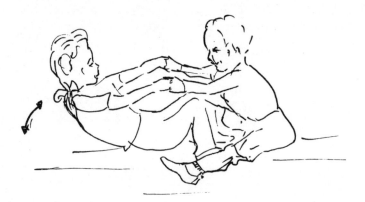

Child lying on his back
Bring your child up from a lying position and down again to the rhythm of a song, slowly enough for him to raise his head and raise himself. Hold his wrists or grasp his hands. Children enjoy doing this facing each other as well as sitting one behind the other.

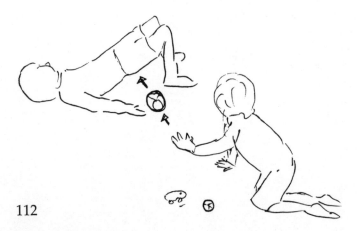

Play holding his feet flat, knees bent, and raising up his hips so that a ball or a noisy car can be pushed underneath him. Teach him the words 'under your hips', if he can understand this concept. Lying flat, help him reach his toes to play with them.

Rolling
Your child may enjoy being rolled over and over in a blanket suspended by two family members. Children can take turns to roll down inclined mattresses or, outdoors, down grassy banks. Continue to encourage your child to turn and reach towards your face or for a toy. He then learns to roll over in order to reach what he wants. Place the toy first at his side, later below and above his face, guiding his reach and roll towards it. At this stage he needs to roll over towards you when you are farther and farther away. By this repeated rolling he comes to understand that the floor is continuous and safe.

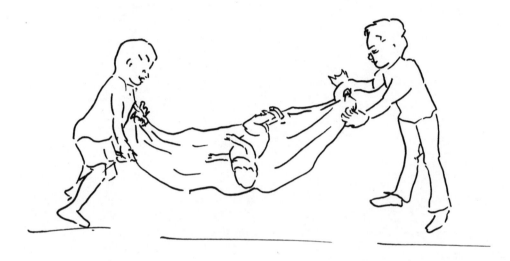

With your child on his back, help him bring his legs over his head. This amuses him and much later he can be helped along further into a somersault. Take care of his head as you do this! He can also play with his feet now that he lifts his legs up.

Child sitting with less and less support

Give your child less and less support with your body and hold his body with your hands on his waist, then his hips and then just his thighs or feet. Move his body away from leaning against the table and progress to having him grasp a support with only one hand, until finally he sits without any supports. Challenge his balance in all these ways as he plays.

Sit him across your body when you are on the floor. Tip him from side to side to fall playfully onto cushions and later all the way to the floor. Place his hand down so that he can catch his balance on it and also discover the floor. You may do this with him sitting on the floor and tipping him forward, backward, to each side and in diagonal directions as a game of 'find the floor'.

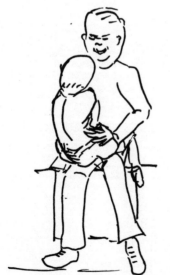

Sit your child across your lap and tip him from side to side facing you and then facing a mirror or window with a clear vertical frame. Wait for him to adjust his head and body to the upright. Also tilt him in these 'see-saw' games towards the front and back. Go slowly and well into the next stages for him to develop confidence and control of his posture.

If he struggles and cries or grabs your clothes, he may not be ready for this postural control. First, gently build up his confidence by bouncing and swaying him a little, giving him more body support. Use a song for both your pleasure and his.

Your child now plays while sitting and is reaching out in all directions for toys he can see, hear and smell. Also lift one of his knees up and outward so that you can play with his toes on his lap.

Bottom-shuffling (scooting)

Once your child can control being tilted and can catch his balance on his hands, he has confidence to shuffle along the floor in a sitting posture. Show him how to do this by sitting next to him and tilting his bottom forward and along the floor.

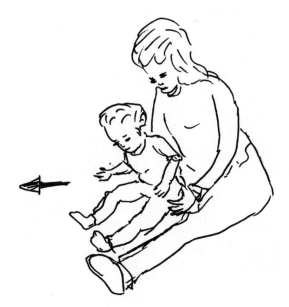

Sitting coming up to standing

Hold his upper arms, then his forearms and later grasp his hands. Bring him well forward so that he stands up and sits down again to a slow rhythm. Make sure both his feet are held flat on the ground and that his face moves well forward over his feet as he comes up to standing. He plays 'up and down' with another child holding his hands and doing the same actions. In the next stages he can get up to standing without help.

Your child may be able to stand leaning against your lap or between your knees as you talk and play with him. Sway him gently from one foot to the other, keeping his head and body upright. Do this with him against a wall, swaying him forward into your arms or playfully pushing you away. He will benefit from spending much time in correct standing postures at play at sandpits, water tables or other tables of toys. His standing needs to be well established before you begin stepping.

Encourage him to stand while holding on to a sturdy toy trolley, box or kitchen chair. Your physiotherapist may also suggest a special walking aid. Once he has acquired some standing stability, your child is helped to take steps with any of these walking aids. See next stage for 'Walking', p. 125.

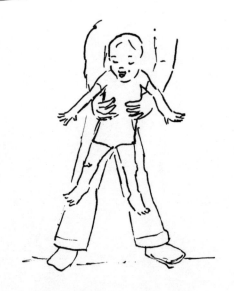

Increase your child's confidence by lifting him up into the air and lowering him to the floor with a happy sound. Wait for him to spread his legs in anticipation of landing on the floor. If he cannot do so, ask someone to guide his legs outwards. This should not be done with children who have very stiff, spastic legs or who do not have sensation in their legs.

Using Hands

Find play activities which develop hand actions in the following general developmental order. Try all these hand actions in the different postures according to your child's abilities. Encourage him to keep looking as he completes hand activities.

Bringing hand to mouth holding an object for exploring by mouthing. Mouthing decreases as you develop the other hand actions with your child.

Bringing hands to other body parts, other arm, hand and later to feet. For example, he strokes other parts of his body, pulls bangles on and off as well as Mum's and Dad's big socks, shoes or paper bags. Help him search and find your mouth, nose and other body parts.

Using both hands at the same time
- If one hand is more impaired, encourage him to hold the toy with it as he explores with the other hand.
- Give him large toys or boxes to hold with two hands.
- Place the same size ball, cube or handle of a rattle in each hand at the same time. Not only does he then use his hands equally but he hears the same sound and feels the same texture or shape on each side.
     This prepares him for future understanding that objects are the same. Progress to his banging the objects together and on each side of the table, first under your guidance and then on his own. He then hears the different sounds he makes with various objects. Now offer him two differently shaped, textured or sound-making toys to hold, and later bang them in a similar way.
- Passing objects from one hand to the other can bring hands together.
- Arrange games which need the actions of one hand after the other, such as when playing drums or the xylophone and when dropping objects one after the other onto a noisy surface.
- Encourage him to accompany songs by clapping his hands together or onto your body or onto his own body.

Reaching out to touch, pat, or get hold of any interesting object. Encourage reaching in all directions, expecting your child to maintain his balance in sitting, kneeling or standing positions.

Letting go of a toy may first be possible if he presses it against a firm surface. Perhaps he will let go if you press down on top of his hand. You may have to pull his thumb gently out from its base to open his tightly closed hand.

Placing or letting go into a large container onto a noisy table or into your hand and onto your lap. Once he can let go he can pass a toy from hand to hand as well.

Picking up, placing and letting go develops from earlier actions you have already used.

NOTE: All such letting go actions help to decrease the tendency to throw wildly. Throwing wildly is usual with a child who cannot see or understand the reason for placing objects down or into containers.

Using hands to search and find when his vision is very poor
Guide your child to find what he has dropped or let go. Show him a systematic way of feeling along the surface to find a toy. Leave his hand free to search and only guide his arm. Later show him how to slide and feel along the edges of tables, toys and containers, as well as any special aids he needs to use.

Developing separate use of fingers
Develop the use of each finger and thumb through playing with his fingers in his mouth, in food or in a bowl of sand, lentils or dried peas. He can touch a knob, small toy or matchbox which then makes a nice sound or rolls away. Use toys, telephones, rings, ribbons and strings on fingers, or any way you know to arouse his interest in using his fingers.

You have to hold his other fingers to help him point out his index or second finger or thumb. Also pat his fingertips together and on tables and toys to make attractive sounds.

Pointing a finger to indicate a toy he wants is very difficult for him if he cannot see very well.

Holding smaller and smaller toys and natural objects from his home, the garden and the countryside.

Picking up and emptying containers
Help your child hold bowls, boxes or small baskets of toys or other unbreakable objects. He will love turning out all the contents and then picking up, grasping and putting each one back again. This allows him to practise all the hand actions you have been developing.

Grasping and turning the hand
This is important when a child is looking and discovering what an object looks like from various angles. Try this in different postures of his body or of his whole arm as his hand may be too stiff to turn. You may first have to turn his whole arm from his shoulder or from his elbow without forcing it, and also press his thumb out from its base to relax his tight hand.

Hand movements to songs will help his play. Examples of these are:
- Hand flat on a slippery surface or in sand. Open and close fingers.
- Fists on the table. Stretch and bend fingers.
- 'Roly-Poly'. Place his forearms and hands on a table and help him to roll them outwards and inwards. Shiny stick-on pictures on each palm may attract his interest.
- Fists on a table, point or stretch out index finger and then other fingers. Fists on table facing each other, point index finger out, then other fingers.

Looking

Continue playing as in First Stages, encouraging him to look at you more as you move about and are farther away from him. As he uses his hands with smaller and smaller objects make sure he has time to look at them against a contrasting background. Offer toys more to each side, above and below him. Later try to help him look at a toy behind him. Encourage him to move and find a toy he wants at a distance at which he can just see it. Practise looking from one toy to another placed at different distances apart or at different distances away from him.

Listening

When you are together and quiet, play listening for your voice not only in front of him but also from where he cannot see you. Touch and turn him gently at first to each side, then below and above, and much later behind him to find you as you keep talking. Do this with a toy that keeps buzzing or playing music. Later make a sound and wait for him to find it once it does not continue all the time. Keep it a game and give him the toy or greet him happily when he succeeds in finding you.

Sensing

Continue as in First Stages, gradually introducing more and more ideas. Gently turn your child to look towards where you touch him with your hands, a toy or a bag of strong-smelling herbs. Touch and kiss, blow and put a vibrating toy on various parts of his body for him to find. Hang a ring of bells on his foot and help him find that.

Communicating

Continue the activities of First Stages. If you show what a toy can do, repeat this many times and guide him. Repeat this again and also see if he anticipates what will happen next. Children love knocking over a tower of bricks or pressing a knob which results in something amusing, as with a Jack-in-the-Box. Only you will get tired with the many times all this will be repeated for his amusement! However, take care not to alarm a blind baby with a sudden loud clatter. He may begin to understand some words which say what you are doing, which parts of his body you are touching, his name, Mummy, Daddy, or yes and no. Always precede actions with the same phrase, such as 'Up you come!' when you pick him up for play. He uses gestures in this and into the next stages. For example, he points if he can see, he pushes you away, pulls you towards a toy or gives you a kiss. You can teach him such actions.

Understanding

All actions for using hands are particularly interwoven with a child's understanding in this and the next stages. Container play should be varied with different-sized containers, different-sized objects and having the containers in different places in front, at the side, above and below your child. His moving and control of posture develops as part of such play activities as well.

'Find the Toy' may be started at the end of this stage and into the next. It is particularly difficult to understand for children with multiple disabilities but needs development. Partly hide the toy under a see-through cloth or plastic bowl. Guide his arm so that his hand finds the toy. Then half-cover and finally fully cover the toy so that he becomes more able to find it. If his vision is very poor, use a continuously buzzing toy, musical box or alarm clock to assist him to find them under the cover. This game alerts your child to the idea that when something is hidden from sight it continues to exist, despite not being seen.

120

'*Where Are You?*' Have a cloth to cover your face and later his face and play finding each other. Progress into the next stages playing 'Peek-a-Boo' games like this with your hands and hiding behind furniture. Your child is learning that though you disappear you continue to exist.

The continuity of the floor is being understood by your child through his rolling, creeping, crawling and bottom-shuffling about. However, to help him understand that the floor does remain continuous and that he will not fall off, play other games as well. Place him on a blanket, preferably on his side or on his stomach over a pillow. Now slide him about in all directions and across the room. Also push him around on wheeled trolleys, prone trolleys or tricycles.

Socialising within family gatherings or groups of other children is important for your child if these gatherings are not too boisterous. He needs to hear laughing, talking and people addressing him as well as each other by name. Names are initially easier to understand than he/she, they/we or you/me.

He may still have a strong attachment to his main carer, preferring him or her to be near when he meets new friends and relations.

Controlling Posture and Moving

Changing positions

Show your child how to push on his hands to get onto boxes, chairs and couches. He may find this way of moving useful for bottom-shuffling upstairs or, if he is going to have a wheelchair, to get into the wheelchair. Some children can transfer this way from chair to bed. He can also develop the ability to stand up from a chair without help.

Encourage him to change his positions to find what he sees, hears or smells on tables, under chairs and in open cardboard boxes. Naturally, have strong-smelling foods in places where they are usually kept so as not to confuse him. You need to help a child with poor vision feel along the legs and seats of chairs or couches before he gets onto them. Whatever way *he* chooses to climb on is also important.

Balance control for sitting increases if your child can have a ride on someone's shoulders. Perhaps he can ride on your back or enjoy riding a pony. Swings and other play equipment in a playground are a great help if you introduce them gradually and with much support.

Standing alone

Some children may have started doing this at the end of the last stage, but most take longer to achieve it. You can help your child to stand during play by holding him between your knees and slowly removing the support of your knees against his hips. Sing to him, play clap hands or both of you hold a toy, to distract him from a fear of falling. Continue to offer him play activities when he is standing at a sand-tray, water bowl or table of toys. Remember to watch that he has his feet flat and apart, with his weight taken equally through each leg. Use both his arms to encourage his head and body to stay in the middle. Sway him from foot to foot to a song when he has sufficient balance control for this.

Standing and catching his balance with a step

Hold your child's hips and sway him suddenly forwards so he takes a little step to stop himself from falling. Also, tip him from side to side or at an angle so that he takes a little step. Later he achieves this response of stepping on being tipped backwards. Make a game of it—perhaps he can push you over? Holding his body, tip him downwards towards a chair and then to the ground. As he learnt in the last stage, he will put his hands down to catch his balance. Show him how far it is to chairs and how far it is to the floor.

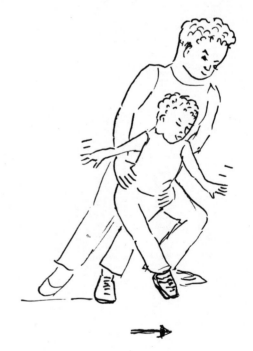

123

Standing, lifting one leg
Play with him at lifting his leg forwards, sideways and then backwards in such games as kicking dangling bells, kicking a noisy tin can or a ball. At first he may need to control his balance by placing his foot on a toy on wheels, a large ball or a box. He can then push these objects away as well as step over them. Stepping onto and off a sturdy box develops his ability to climb stairs. At first both his hands are held and then one. Some children need to have their elbows straight and their weight brought forward so that they do not lean or fall backwards.

Standing and reaching in all directions
This is developed as he hits a dangling toy or balloons, or is attracted to something on a shelf. You may guide him to stand and throw a cushion and balls of different sizes. He can do this with other children. He will probably find it much more difficult to catch a ball if his vision is poor and his co-ordination undeveloped, but he may still gain this skill much later, so place his arms out in readiness for a ball. Let someone warn him and gently throw a cushion or ball into his arms. All these ball games improve his balance and stimulate him to sway on his legs, which he will need for future walking.

REMEMBER: Ask your therapist if your child needs special shoes, calipers or splints for standing. If so you will be shown how to put them on correctly.

Stepping sideways (cruising)

Help him do this from one lap to another person's lap. Also use the wall or a couch and other furniture.

Walking

This may be started in this stage with some children, using the walking aids mentioned in the last stage. He first walks with you holding his arms in front or by grasping a walker, then just grasping a stick, a rope, or toy which you hold. Later he progresses to doing all this without you holding and still later to holding with one hand and, finally, alone. Special walking aids are changed to crutches, quadripod sticks or sticks, according to what your child can be taught to manage. Keep his weight well forward over his feet and do not have him lean back on you. It is important that you continue to practise balance while standing on both feet or one foot as this helps walking patterns. Practise walking on floors where he can hear his own footsteps. (See the illustration of ways of holding his arms and wrists.)

Stairs

He can begin crawling up the stairs and coming down by sliding on his stomach or by sitting and bottom-shuffling down the steps. Show him how to hold the banister and go up sideways, or how to go up with both his hands held or with one holding the banisters while you hold his other hand. Let him feel the edge of the step with his foot and place it alone. Stay with him when going up and stand just below him when he begins to go down steps. Going down develops later than going up as it is more difficult. Put a toy on a stair for him to find once he has become more confident about moving on the stairs.

Using Hands

Continue previous stages, especially for finger and thumb play. Show your child how to lift lids off and on pots. Later still he learns to unscrew lids of different-sized containers, and you might leave a little bell or raisin inside the container for him to find. Continue play with containers.

Container play. Your child will already have started letting go of an object into a container to hear the sound and then progressed to taking the object out of that container. He has also put his feet and hands in and out of big shoes, shiny packets—and his mouth! Now you can challenge his understanding and actions more by having:
- Many different-sized containers and different-sized objects.
- Place the containers in different places below, above and to his sides.
- Place the containers in different parts of the room, training his mobility to go to them.
- Have lids on containers so he has to remove them to look for what is inside.
- Teach him to put lids on and take them off.
- Use round and square, tall and small containers with lids.

Your child needs to learn to grasp and pull a ribbon, sticky clay, string or tissue. He also needs to grasp and push a box, his walking aid, a handle of a toy on wheels—and also another person!

Continue activities from Stage Two so that his hand actions become more and more precise.

Looking

Your child can now look farther behind himself to reach a toy you offer. Encourage rolling, crawling, knee-walking or stepping to find a toy he sees farther and farther away. To challenge him, offer him toys that are smaller, do not contrast so much with the colour of his surroundings and are similar in shape to other objects. These challenges depend on his individual abilities.

Listening

Use the same games as for 'Looking'. Your child needs more time to find a toy which makes an interesting sound when it is behind him.

REMEMBER: Hold the toy where it made the sound so that he turns to see it and then reaches to grasp it. Let him play with any toy he makes an effort to reach by moving to get it.

If his head and body balance are still poor he will only be willing to turn and reach if you give him some support.

Sensing

This develops as he uses his hands and whole body together with all his senses in all play activities.

Communicating

Your child may understand a natural gesture and short instruction, and a phrase or word to say what you are going to do. Once he understands play, using his hands and body, talk through some of what you are both doing. However, avoid talking all the time. Special signs for deaf and blind children or those with other problems will be recommended by your teacher or speech therapist. Other children use simple words, gestures and phrases now, but all this is very individual. Words often link with rhythms, movements and play activities. He can now practise taking turns in sounds, playful movements or giving you a toy. He responds to his name, so do use it often.

Understanding

A child's abilities in looking, listening, sensing, use of hands and body are further developed in play activities for understanding. Your child will play pairing, sorting and matching with textures, shapes, smells and sounds according to his own development. His teachers and psychologists will work with both of you to show you how to do this. Useful toys are nesting boxes, large and small rings to fit on a vertical and horizontal stick, large building blocks, toy boxes which can be pulled apart and put together. He will also like toys with moving parts.

Help him play more games of finding a hidden person or a hidden toy (see Second Stages).

Screwing actions of hands can be helped now with lids, large and smaller screwing toys and by turning taps and other household objects. Your child is ready to understand how to do this.

NOTE: Play using fine hand actions together with normal vision is needed for dolls, miniature toys, dolls' house furniture or tiny toy cars. This play develops differently and later than with other children. Discuss this with your child's teacher if your child has severe visual problems.

Ball play

This is of special value for:

- Communication between your child and yourself or other family members.
- For looking from one person to another, for looking at different-sized balls.
- For postural control and moving to fetch the ball, and for hand use.
- Using a ball with a bell helps listening and following a sound.

Catching a ball develops much later due to visual difficulties. Throwing and kicking a ball can be fun for your child earlier in his development.

FOURTH STAGES

Controlling Posture and Moving

Body actions with more use of space, size of own body awareness. Play games with your child, which encourage him to climb into a box, on top of chairs and tables and underneath and behind furniture. He comes to recognise how the size of his body fits into things. Later he can understand the words meaning 'inside', 'outside', 'on top', 'underneath', 'behind'—once he does all these things. All the other actions in this stage widen these experiences. He may:

Walk backwards, sideways, between chairs and people. If he cannot see, begin using his hands to search where he walks.

Stand and balance as he picks up objects on the floor, on a box or from inside a basket or container. He likes to feel his head and body upside down and see the world upside down.

Tricycle with pedals or his feet walking along the ground across an open space first before he learns to go between chairs or through doors.

Go up stairs two feet per stair and down stairs with less support of banister and holding your hand. Going down is more difficult than going up. Go up sideways, facing the banister.

Walk across different floor surfaces, rough ground and inclines. This is guided, with your child being shown how to use his foot to feel unknown areas. Also practise feeling along a path with his foot to check the direction of the path, if he cannot see it.

Running can be guided by holding his hand and by the child holding lightly to a long rope tied across a space between two poles. A pathway for walking and running should have such a rope.

Pushing or pulling large toys as he walks is something a child enjoys. Also, if he pushes someone in a wheelchair or on a trike it is fun for both people

Continue having your child stand on one foot and balance as he kicks a dangling noisy toy or ball, or pushes a rattly car or ball along the ground to someone. He stands on one foot and steps over a number of large, bright toys as well as walking around and between them.

NOTE: Children at this stage of understanding may be unaware of danger. If they also have severe visual impairment there needs to be extra training in detecting and avoiding hazards. All children at these stages must be helped to learn their limitations for safety. Advice and suggestions from mobility instructors of people with severe visual impairment is important.

Using Hands, Looking, Listening, Sensing, Communicating and Understanding

These are more and more interwoven during play activities, such as:

Picking up a variety of smaller and smaller objects and toys.

Feeling edges of more differently-shaped toys which are not too complicated for your particular child.

Exploring any moving parts, pulling them apart and putting them together again. Do check the safety of toys and objects used.

Letting go more precisely into your hand and into many differently-sized containers. Placing large and smaller-sized pegs or other shapes into their correct holes is associated with such actions. Post-box toys and other formboards help your child's development now.

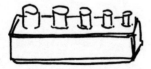

Feeling and putting in different shapes into holes, boxes and cylinders usually focuses on circles, squares and triangles at first. A child with very poor sight needs some guidance with feeling the shaped openings before experimenting with which shape will go into what.

Screwing actions with large and finer screw-toys and lids of different sizes interest him now.

Turning handles, doorknobs, taps and using different switches may attract him. Switching on and off lights and music is a well-known joy for a child.

Crumpling, squeezing, tearing and folding paper of many different textures is also fun and teaches him much of value.

Scribbling is more used by those who can see. However, a blind or partially sighted child can draw in sand and feel his imprint there.

Large bead threading and fitting a variety of large and small rings onto thick, thin, wooden or rope sticks are important in play. Hold stick or rope in the vertical, horizontal or diagonal positions so that he can gain greater experience in the use of all his abilities.

Water play and sand play are great situations for pouring and filling jugs and containers of all sizes. Strainers and spades of various sizes will increase these play activities for him.

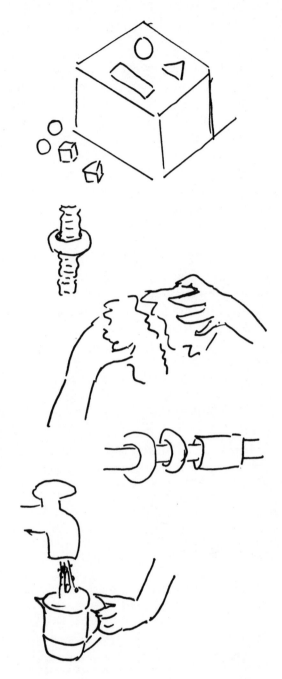

'Give me' and other simple phrases emerge naturally from play. Your child takes turns in play and also learns to choose from more than one activity or from more than two or three toys. So exploring and learning generate communication in many ways.

Pretend play or imaginative play

These forms of play develop differently in children with different abilities. You may have to make the initial suggestions for pretend play, like 'shopping', 'cooking' or pretending to do things like Mummy or Daddy. As soon as possible give your child time and space to continue his own ideas and develop new ways of representing what he knows of his world and what he is struggling to understand about it.

Children may now use the objects which they explored in earlier stages for pretend play. A container may become a hat; perhaps his walking aid becomes a bus or car. Shells, stones or leaves may become food for cooking in a container or serving at a tea party for his friends. Such pretending depends on how a child has perceived his world, and himself in that world, in the context of his own abilities and disabilities. His play with a doll, dolls' house or other small toys will be different from that of an able-bodied child and your intervention should be minimal. You, of course, provide the material and the toys, and you should respond to your child when invited to do so and not direct his play.

Pets

Animals or birds provide a child with emotional satisfactions as well as with sounds, smells and scenes of great interest. A blind child needs to know what, say, barks and how such an animal feels in texture and shape. You can bring this to him. Of course children in earlier stages do not appreciate the dangers of handling animals incorrectly, so do teach that for safety reasons.

Helping adults and other children

At this and later stages children like being helpful at home and at school. Find little tasks for your child and appreciate his contribution. Working together with you during a household task matters for the special intimacy it creates between you. Opportunities can be given for speech, and communication grows. Your child also uses his abilities in sensing, balancing, moving and using his hands while carrying out these tasks. He will feel part of your family and part of the social group at school.

Communicating with Controlling Posture and Moving

Your child enjoys rhymes, chants and other rhythmic songs. Use these with controlling posture and moving activities.

He will also be able to touch a number of body parts if asked. Use this ability together with moving and using hands.

Understanding simple directions and 'in', 'under', 'on top', 'behind', 'along' and other words also links with movement activities at this stage.

Using people's names. As you always used his name, he now knows you are talking to him and responds to his own name. Teach him names of more people. He will find his own way of recognising them. Small group play activity with other children helps him develop these and other social interactions.

PETER

Peter can sit well, kneel upright and stand alone while playing at a table. However, he refuses to walk with anyone or push a trolley of bricks. He is very good with his hands and uses his looking and listening abilities well when toys are very near to him. Most of the time he persuades people to take him in his wheelchair or carry him about. He dislikes lying on the floor and always indicates his desire to be at a table with other children or with toys.

His carer now begins to develop his understanding that the floor is safe and continuous. On the floor she sits behind him holding his body and helps him tilt from side to side and shuffle forwards. She also holds him over her arm and helps him crawl forwards or roll along the floor. Together with other children lying on a blanket, she and a much older child drag them along the ground for a joyful ride. She places nearby his favourite toys which make sounds and glitter, and then slides them farther and farther away. Together they bottom-shuffle and crawl to find them.

After many other games along the floor, Peter develops his understanding and wants to move himself. The carer and other members of his family now walk with him across the floor as often as he is willing to go and find his toys and someone he likes. They persuade him to do this after he chooses to go to what appeals to him. In time his walking becomes more fun and everyone shares his pleasure.

Once Peter has made the effort to reach his toy he is of course given time to play with it.

JOANNA

Joanna likes to lie on her side watching and listening to others playing. Her arms and legs are usually bent in this position when lying on her back or on her stomach. In sitting and standing she bends over and often falls forwards. She likes watching lights and people moving about. When lying down she turns to sounds but does not move towards them. She is passive during all daily activities, enjoying being looked after, tickled, massaged and played with like a helpless baby. She is five years old.

Her carer now tries to develop the next stages of play. She develops her control of posture sitting in a chair with her hands placed flat on the table and elbows straight. Joanna stretches one of her knees and is guided to kick the table, making a noise which amuses her. Her carer also hangs mobiles above her and guides her arm to touch and so stretch out to pat them. This stimulates her to raise her head to see the shiny and tinkling mobiles. This game is also played with her stretched out on a wedge lying on her stomach. As she stretches her arm to pat the mobile she begins her own play. All this stretching helps her overcome her usual bent postures.

Joanna is encouraged to reach out for dangling mobiles over her bath, over her bed and later when she is stretched out on a prone standing apparatus. Much later, when lying on the floor with a small cushion under her chest, she pushes a dangling bell towards another child in front of her. This child pushes it back to her and play continues for a short time. The child goes away and she watches her move away and begins to move in a creeping fashion along the floor to follow this child. This is observed by a carer who gives a shiny ball to this child to give Joanna after she has crept forwards.

But Joanna needs some physical guidance to show her how to creep as her own efforts are not adequate. This is practised with her many times. Each time she reaches the shiny ball by creeping, she is given it to play with.

10 MOVING FROM PLACE TO PLACE

Many people feel that walking is a separate activity which should be trained on its own. This is only partly true. As we discussed in Chapter 1, walking depends on all the basic abilities which are developed in the daily living activities. Let us look more closely at walking to increase our understanding of the direct connections between it and any daily activity.

Watch yourself take a slow, normal step. Which abilities of controlling posture and moving are you using? Normally you are:

- Holding your head up.
- Holding your body upright.
- Taking your weight through your legs and feet.
- Swaying yourself slightly to one side so that one leg is freed to take a step.
- Swaying yourself forward so that you take the step.
- Balancing on one leg as your other leg takes the step.
- Swinging your arms when your balance is controlled but reaching out and holding on when your balance is difficult.

Your child may already have achieved one or other of these abilities; it will depend on her own stages of development. You can then see which of the remaining abilities she still needs to achieve. The methods you can use for this are those that you are already using during daily activities. Examples are: your child holding her head up when she looks and communicates with you during feeding, playing or other activities; your child holding her body upright when she sits on her potty, on your lap and during washing, dressing, eating and play; your child swaying from side to side or forward as she puts out her arm or leg for dressing, washing and playing. Finally, when she stands, balancing on one leg while she lifts her foot to be washed, dried or have a sock or shoe put on, she is also gaining the balance on one leg needed for walking.

Using Hands

Your child will need to use her hands rather more for holding on than a child without her difficulties. She will need to reach out and grasp, lean on her hands and grasp and let go of supports during her efforts to learn to walk. She will need to hold on more than other children when developing sitting, kneeling and standing postures. These upright positions all develop balance for walking. She will also use her hands to push or pull large playthings on wheels, special walking aids and people while learning to walk.

So you see, all that you are doing together during daily activities to develop use of her hands contributes to the achievement of walking.

Walking and Daily Activities

Besides developing all the abilities of head and body control, balance and using hands in different daily activities, you need to bring them together in the act of walking itself. Practical ideas are given in all the activities, especially in play. Learning to walk then has a purpose for your child and is also pleasurable.

It is important to make time for your child to practise walking as she goes from one daily activity to another. She will do this when she is ready for it according to her stages of development.

Specialised treatments
Your doctors and therapists will add to your observations of your child's abilities. In individual children specialised procedures and treatment sessions may be planned.

Positions used in daily activities
The different positions of lying, sitting and standing used in daily activities lead to various ways of getting from place to place. Your child may roll, creep, crawl or walk on her knees in preparation for walking. However, even if she cannot achieve walking, these other ways of getting around allow her to feel more independent.

Her control of posture and moving, together with use of her hands gained during daily activities, helps her find methods of getting out of bed, turning over in bed and moving from bed to other places. If she has a wheelchair she can use these and other basic abilities to transfer to other chairs, baths, showers, or other situations.

Let's look at the positions used in daily activities to see how they lead to a number of possible ways of moving from place to place.

Child lying on her side leads to rolling. She can also turn over in bed and later pull herself up to sitting. From sitting she can get out of bed.

Child lying on her stomach leads to rolling, creeping, crawling, walking on hands with her body supported on a board or wedge on castors. She may get up to kneeling and step on her knees along furniture or with a chair. Getting out of bed may be achieved by rolling and getting up to sit followed by standing up. Perhaps she may slide herself off the bed onto her knees or use another method of her own.

Child lying on her back also leads to rolling and getting up to sit and then to getting out of bed.

Child sitting leads to shuffling on her bottom. She may use her sitting ability in wheelchairs, on tricycles, on playground equipment which transports her along the ground. Sitting on a pony or horse offers her another way of getting from place to place.

Child standing leads to stepping sideways along furniture or the wall. Standing leads to walking forwards. Later she walks backwards up and down inclined floors and steps.

Other ways of moving from place to place
Your child may use her own ways of getting around which are undesirable because they cause deformities. Usually the deformities are caused when only one way of getting around is used frequently. For example, she may drag herself on stiffly bent arms and press her legs tightly together as she moves along the floor. Another child may slide herself along the floor by stiffening her head back and arching her body. Other children crawl by hopping with both knees together and twisting their arms inward as they take their weight through clenched fists. Some adults hold a child under her armpits as she steps on her toes, crossing her ankles or excessively bending her knees.

Ask your therapist whether your child's way of moving around is undesirable and what practical ways can be used to deal with it. All the following things can be used:

1   Find many ways for any child to move from place to place instead of only one way.
2   Use a variety of large playthings and special equipment for your child's mobility.
3   Emphasise interesting activities which are done in sitting, kneeling or standing positions. This builds your child's balance so that she can develop a variety of ways of getting about. Choose a position which also corrects the way she repeatedly keeps her arms or legs during an undesirable pattern of moving from place to place. See Chapter 2.
4   Your therapist may suggest additional treatments to overcome the stiffness, weakness or other difficulties which result from an undesirable way of moving about.
5   Take extra care with the correct positions of your child during daily activities. Suggestions on how to position her are given in Chapters 5–9.

Using Wheelchairs and Equipment

You will have to teach your child how to get in and out of any equipment. Give time for her to feel the equipment with her hands, slowly accept being placed in it and especially participating in getting in *and* out of the equipment (technical aid), so that she does not feel restricted but rather comes to recognise its value for her mobility.

Using crutches, walking aids and sticks
Once again help her to accept any aids. Crutches and sticks are particularly difficult to use for some children with multiple disabilities and may hamper those with severe visual problems. Experiment with other ways of developing mobility if at all possible.

The use of any walking aids is taught by breaking down the actions into smaller steps. This is discussed in Chapter 2 and the approach given on pages 72 and 91–2. Usually you should physically guide your child from behind and slightly to her side. However, take care she *does not lean back against you* when you are behind her as this prevents her obtaining balance on both feet with her body in the centre. If you speak she may also lean towards your voice for security, so do keep her well onto her own two feet!

Confidence for Moving About

Some children are fearful of learning to walk or to move around in any way. Build your child's confidence by developing her balance and movement at her own pace. Keep the training playful and with a purpose for her. Interest her in finding out how far or near you or a toy is from her so that she gets to know about distance in a playful way. Show her how to save herself from falling by catching herself on her hands or taking a small step with her foot. It is also important for a child with very poor vision to learn how far from the ground she may be, and how far she will fall if she needs to use her saving actions. Of course, you will have to overcome your own fears for her and not convey them to her. Trust her to go at her own pace and she will take care.

Children who have problems with senses of touch or with vision need extra warnings of the hazards that they may face. It is helpful to ask a mobility instructor for blind people to suggest more ideas for your own child with severe visual impairment.

REMEMBER that walking may take many years to develop in some children. If it does not ultimately develop, it is still possible for a person who cannot walk to enjoy a rich and fulfilled life in a wheelchair.

CHRISTINA

Christina takes time to be placed on her carer's lap as she stiffens and twists backwards. She prefers just to remain lying on her back and feels fearful of new postures. After being held sitting and bent forwards at her hips with her arms on a table and her feet safely flat on a surface during eating, playing and being dried after washing, she begins to sit with her carer's support and with the reassurance of being close to the body of her carer. After a while she enjoys being bounced on her bottom on her carer's lap and this stimulates her to hold her head up and even to begin to hold up her upper body as her carer supports her at her waist and hips.

After more months Christina accepts being tipped farther and farther over to each side and also towards the front and backwards. She is encouraged to adjust or bend her body towards an upright sitting posture so that she does not fall. Meanwhile her carer plays with her sitting on the floor and falling to each side and forwards to catch her balance onto her arms and hands. She does this rather better than just adjusting her body to stop falling, but both ways give her more confidence and control.

USEFUL ADDRESSES

ACT (Access to Communication and Technology), Oak Tree Lane Centre, Oak Tree Lane, Selly Oak, Birmingham B29 6JA. Tel/Fax: 0121 627 8235. Email:actcomtec@aol.com

Action for Sick Children, 300 Kingston Road, London SW20 8LX. Tel: 020 8542 4848. Fax: 020 8542 2424. Email: action/4/6/children/edu@msn.com

AFASIC (Association for All Speech Impaired Children), 69–85 Old Street, London EC1V 9HX. Helpline: 020 7236 3632. Website: http://www.afasic.org.uk

Association for Spina Bifida and Hydrocephalus, 209 Crescent Road, New Barnet, Herts EN4 8SB. Tel: 020 8449 0475. Fax: 020 8440 6168. Email: jof@asbah.demon.co.uk. Website: http://www.asbah.demon.co.uk

Barnardo's, Tanner Lane, Barkingside, Ilford, Essex IG6 1QG. Tel: 020 8550 8822. Fax: 020 8551 6870. Website: http://www.barnados.org.uk

British Association of Occupational Therapists (*for current address of specialist National Association of Paediatric Occupational Therapists*), 106–111 Borough High Street, London SE1 1LB. Tel: 020 7357 6480. Fax: 020 7450 2290.

Capabalities Scotland (previously called Scottish Council for Spastics), 22 Corstorphine Road, Edinburgh EH12 6HP. Tel: 0131 337 9876. Fax: 0131 346 7864. Email: capability@capability-scotland.org.uk. Website: http://www.capability-scotland.org.uk

Chartered Society of Physiotherapy (*specialist groups: Association of Paediatric Chartered Physiotherapists and Association of Physiotherapists interested in Neurology*), 14 Bedford Row, London WC1R 4ED. Tel: 020 7242 1941. Fax: 020 7306 6611. Email: csp@csphysio.org.uk. Website: http://www.csp.org.uk

Children's Legal Centre, University of Essex, Wivenhoe Park, Colchester, Essex CO4 3SQ. Tel: 01206 873820.

College of Speech and Language Therapists, 2 White Hart Yard, London SE1 1NX. Tel: 020 7378 1200. Fax: 020 7403 7254. Email: postmaster@rcslt.org.uk Website: http://www.rcslt.org.uk

Communication Advice Centre, Musgrave Park Hospital, Stockman's Lane, Belfast BT9 7JB. Tel: 02890 669501. Fax: 02890 683662 (*Centre for advice on communication aids.*)

Contact a Family, 170 Tottenham Court Road, London W1P 0HA. Tel: 020 7383 3555. Fax: 020 7383 0259. Email: info@cafamily.org.uk. Website: http://www.cafamily.org.uk

Crossroads Care Attendant Scheme, National Office, 10 Regent Place, Rugby, Warwickshire CV21 2PN. Tel: 01788 573653. Fax: 01788 565498

CRY-SIS, BM CRY-SIS, 27 Old Gloucester Street, London WC1N 3XX. Tel: 020 7404 5011. (*Support group for parents of crying babies.*)

Disabled Living Foundation, 380/384 Harrow Road, London W9 2HU. Helpline: 0870 603 9177. Tel: 020 7289 6111. Fax: 020 7266 2922. Email: info@dlf.org.uk. Website: http://www.dlf.org.uk

Down's Syndrome Association, 153 Mitcham Road, Tooting, London SW17 9PG. Tel: 020 8682 4001. Fax: 020 8682 4012. Website: http://www.downs-syndrome.org.uk

Headway (National Head Injuries Association), 4 King Edward Court, King Edward Street, Nottingham NG1 1EW. Tel: 0115 924 0800. Fax: 0115 958 4446. Email: enquiries@headway.org.uk. Website: http://www.headway.org.uk

Hyperactive Children's Support Group, 71 Whyke Lane, Chichester, West Sussex PO19 2LD. Tel: 01903 725182

ISSAC (UK) Communication Matters. (Administration): The ACE Centre, 92 Windmill Road, Headington, Oxford OX3 7DR. Tel: 01865 763 508

KIDSACTIVE, Pryor's Bank, Bishops Park, London SW6 3LA. Tel: 020 7731 1435. Fax: 020 7731 4426. Email: ntis@kidsactive.org.uk (information service). Website: http://www.kidsactive.org.uk

MENCAP (Royal Society for Mentally Handicapped Children and Adults), 123 Golden Lane, London EC1Y 0RT. Tel: 020 7454 0454. Fax: 020 7608 3254. Email: info@mencap.org.uk. Website: http://www.mencap.org.uk

Microcephalic Support Group, 22 Auctioneers Court, Auctioneers Way, The Old Cattle Market, Northampton NN1 1EY. Tel: 01604 603743

Muscular Dystrophy Group of Great Britain and N. Ireland, 7/11 Prescott Place, London SW4 6BS. Tel: 020 7720 8055. Fax: 020 7498 0670. Email: info@muscular-dystrophy.org. Website: http://www.muscular-dystrophy.org.uk

National Deaf Children's Society, National Office: 15 Dufferin Street, London EC1Y 8PD. Tel: 020 7250 0123 (V/T); Parent's Helpline 2pm–5pm: 0800 252380. Fax: 020 7251 5020. Email: ndcs@ndcs.org.uk

National Association for Toy and Leisure Libraries, 68 Churchway, London NW1 1LT. Tel: 020 7387 9592. Fax: 020 7383 2714. Email: admin@natll.ukf.net. Website: http://www.charitynet.org/~NATLL

PHAB (*Physically handicapped and able-bodied clubs*), Summit House, Wandle Road, Croydon CR0 1DF. Tel: 020 8667 9443. Fax: 020 8681 1399. Email: phab@ukonline.co.uk. Website: http://www.ukonline.co.uk/phab

Pre-School Learning Alliance, 61 Kings Cross Road, London WC1X 9LL. Tel: 020 7833 0991. Fax: 020 7837 4942. Email: pla@pre-school.org.uk

RNIB (Royal National Institute for the Blind), 224 Great Portland Street, London W1N 6AA. Tel: 020 7388 1266. Fax: 020 7383 4921

RNID (Royal National Institute for Deaf People), 19–23 Featherstone Street, London EC1Y 8SL. Tel: 020 7296 8000. Fax: 020 7296 8199. Minicom: 020 7296 8001

Riding for the Disabled Association, Avenue R, National Agricultural Centre, Kenilworth, Warwickshire CV8 2LY. Tel: 01203 696510. Fax: 01203 696532

SENSE (National Association for Deaf-Blind), 11–13 Clifton Terrace, Finsbury Park, London N4 3SR. Tel: 020 7272 7774. Fax: 020 7272 6012. Minicom: 020 727 9848. Email: sense@sense.org.uk

SCOPE (for people with cerebral palsy), 6 Market Road, London N7 9PW. Tel: 020 7636 5020. Fax: 020 7619 7399

SCTCI (Scottish Centre of Technological Communication of the Impaired), Westmarc, Southern General Hospital, 1345 Govan Road, Glasgow G51 4TF. Tel: 0141 201 2619

FURTHER READING

Barrett, J. *Help Me Speak: A Parent's Guide to Speech and Language Therapy*, 1994, Souvenir Press.

Clarke, P., Kofsky, H., and Laurvol, J. *To A Different Drumbeat*, 1989, Hawthorn Press.

Cunningham, C. *Down's Syndrome: An Introduction for Parents*, 2nd ed. 1988, Souvenir Press.

Finnie, N. *Handling the Young Cerebral Palsied Child at Home*, 1974, Heinemann.

Goldschmied, E., and Jackson, S. *People under Three: Young Children in Day Care*, 1994, Routledge.

Griffiths, M., and Russell, P. (eds.). *Working Together with Handicapped Children: Guidelines for parents and professionals*, 1985, Souvenir Press.

Griffiths, M., and Clegg, M. *Cerebal Palsy: Problems and Practice*, 1988, Souvenir Press.

Jeffree, D. M., McConkey, R., and Hewson, S. *Let Me Play*, 2nd ed. 1985, Souvenir Press.

Lear, R. *Play Helps: Toys and Activities for Handicapped Children*, 1977, Heinemann.

McConkey, R., and Jeffree, D. M. *Let's Make Toys*, 1981, Souvenir Press.

Newson, E., and Hipgrave, T. *Getting Through to Your Handicapped Child*, 1982, Cambridge University Press.

Stanton, M. *Cerebral Palsy*, 1992, Options.

Scott, E. P., Jan, J. E., and Freeman, D. *Can't Your Child See?*, 1977, University Park Press, Baltimore and London.

Sonkson, P., and Stiff, B. *Show Me What My Friends Can See*, 1991, Developmental Vision Clinic, The Wolfson Centre, Mecklenburgh Square, London WC1N 2AP.

Wyman, R. *Multiply Handicapped Children*, 1986, Souvenir Press.

INDEX